The Mayor of Casterbridge

Thomas Hardy

Guide written by
John Mahoney

A *Letts* Literature Guide

Every effort has been made to trace copyright holders and to obtain their permission for the use of copyright material. The author and publishers will gladly receive information enabling them to rectify any reference or credit in subsequent editions.

First published 1994 by BPP (Letts Educational) Ltd, Aldine House, Aldine Place, London W12 8AW

Text © John Mahoney and Stewart Martin 1994

Typeset by Jordan Publishing Design

Self-test questions devised by Hilary Lissenden

Text design Jonathan Barnard

Cover and text illustrations Hugh Marshall

Graphic illustration Ian Foulis and Associates, Barbara Linton

Design © BPP (Letts Educational) Ltd

All our rights reserved. No part of this publication may be reproduced, stored in a retrieval system, or transmitted, in any form or by any means, electronic, mechanical, photocopying, recording or otherwise, without the prior permission of BPP (Letts Educational) Ltd.

British Library Cataloguing in Publication Data
   Martin, Stewart
    Letts Explore 'The Mayor of Casterbridge': Letts
    Educational Literature Guide
    I. Title II. Mahoney, John
    III. Marshall, Hugh IV. Foulis, Ian
   822.33
   ISBN 1 85758 252 7

Printed and bound in Great Britain by Ashford Colour Press Ltd, Gosport, Hants

Contents

Plot synopsis	5
Characters and themes in *The Mayor of Casterbridge*	6
Who's who in *The Mayor of Casterbridge*	10
Themes in *The Mayor of Casterbridge*	14
Text commentary Chapters 1–5	16
Self-test questions and answers Chapters 1–5	21
Text commentary Chapters 6–12	23
Self-test questions and answers Chapters 6–12	29
Text commentary Chapters 13–22	31
Self-test questions and answers Chapters 13–22	41
Text commentary Chapters 23–33	43
Self-test questions and answers Chapters 23–33	51
Text commentary Chapters 34–45	53
Self-test questions and answers Chapters 34–45	61
Pairings	63
Writing an examination essay	

4

Plot synopsis

Frustrated by his poverty, Michael Henchard blames his troubles on the encumbrances of wife and child. In a drunken moment he 'auctions' his wife, Susan, and baby daughter Elizabeth-Jane to a passing sailor, Newson.

Some nineteen years later, Susan returns to Casterbridge with her daughter to seek Henchard's aid, now that she thinks her sailor 'husband' has been lost at sea. Henchard has become the Mayor of Casterbridge and a successful corn-dealer.

Henchard agrees to court and marry Susan, but neither of them wants Elizabeth-Jane to know they had previously been man and wife, or that Henchard had sold his wife and daughter at auction. Additionally, Susan deceives Henchard about his daughter, because 'his' Elizabeth-Jane had actually died shortly after the auction. This Elizabeth-Jane is, in reality, Newson's daughter.

A stranger, Farfrae, arrives in town, helps Henchard in his corn business, and is appointed manager. The two men become friends. However, events now take a turn for the worse.

Susan dies and Henchard, from a letter she left behind, discovers that Elizabeth-Jane is not his daughter. Bitterly disappointed, he rejects her, but does not have the courage to tell her the reasons why. He falls out with Farfrae, who sets up a corn-business in competition.

Lucetta Templeman, an old love of Henchard's, settles in the town and falls in love with Farfrae, who marries her. Henchard's business fails and he is bankrupted. Farfrae buys his business, house and furniture.

Lucetta dies in tragic circumstances. Newson returns and claims his daughter. Farfrae marries Elizabeth-Jane. Henchard, rejected by Elizabeth-Jane, dies alone in poverty, a disillusioned and broken man.

Characters and themes in *The Mayor of Casterbridge*

The story tracks the events in the life of Michael Henchard, the Mayor of Casterbridge. Against his rise and eventual downfall we see the effect he has on Susan, his wife; on Lucetta, a woman whom he once hoped to marry; on Farfrae, his business partner and then rival; and on Elizabeth-Jane, the girl he thought to be his daughter. He is a man of action and great emotion but limited intelligence. His ambition and energy brought him a successful business and the position of mayor. His intemperate nature, jealousy, and inability to cope with personal relationships – to give as well as take – bring about his downfall and death.

Farfrae, a man befriended by Henchard, is intelligent, shrewd, and a canny businessman. He does not really understand Henchard and shows shallowness in his personal relationships. He abandons Elizabeth-Jane as swiftly as he takes up with Lucetta. His wife is not long dead when he again pursues Elizabeth-Jane. He does demonstrate kindness towards Henchard when the latter becomes bankrupt, but he no doubt has his eye on public opinion when he does so.

Susan is a simple woman. Her meekness drives Henchard to distraction, but her determination to provide for Elizabeth-Jane leads her back to Henchard and begins the cycle of his downfall.

Lucetta, like Farfrae, is somewhat shallow in her personal relationships. She rushes into situations, regretting her impulsive actions later.

Elizabeth-Jane is, in many ways, used by the other characters. By hard work and determination, she educates herself and comes to terms with the tragedies which affect her. At the end of the story she is a mentally strong and mature woman.

The setting of the novel in the town of Casterbridge (Dorchester in real life) and in part of the countryside of Wessex (Hampshire and Dorset) is important to the action of the story. The lives of the main characters and their successes and failures are played out against the backdrop of a rural economy which entirely depends on agriculture. The historic setting and details, with their 'past-marked prospect', lend atmosphere to the events of the story and parallel the 'past-marked' events which Henchard, Susan and Lucetta attempt to hide. Hardy's training in architecture shows in the detailed descriptions of buildings and their interiors, helping to make the story's setting and characters seem real and alive.

Important and clear structural devices in the novel give clues to mysteries in the plot, such as the origins of Elizabeth-Jane and the identity of the stranger who appears at the end of the novel. The furmity woman appears at crucial moments for Henchard, and the arrival of Jopp always seems to presage bad news. Duplication of events features frequently: two 'rides', two fights, two lots of five guineas, Henchard's two marriages to Susan, Farfrae's two marriages, two mayors. This symmetry gives the plot a satisfying shape.

Deceptions by Henchard, Susan and Lucetta create secrets that will eventually be disclosed, and bring the tragedy to a head. In many cases, those deceptions lead to, or are accompanied by, loneliness. A wider perspective on the theme of loneliness is given by the travellers who seem to frequent the lonely, dusty roads.

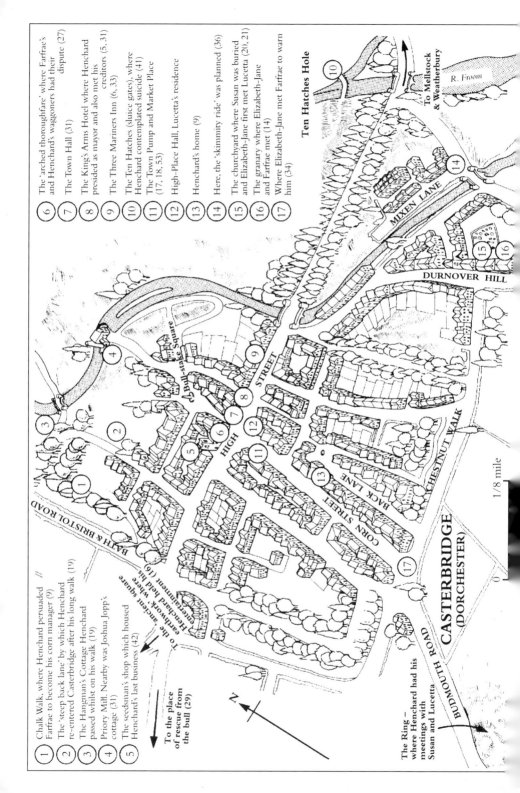

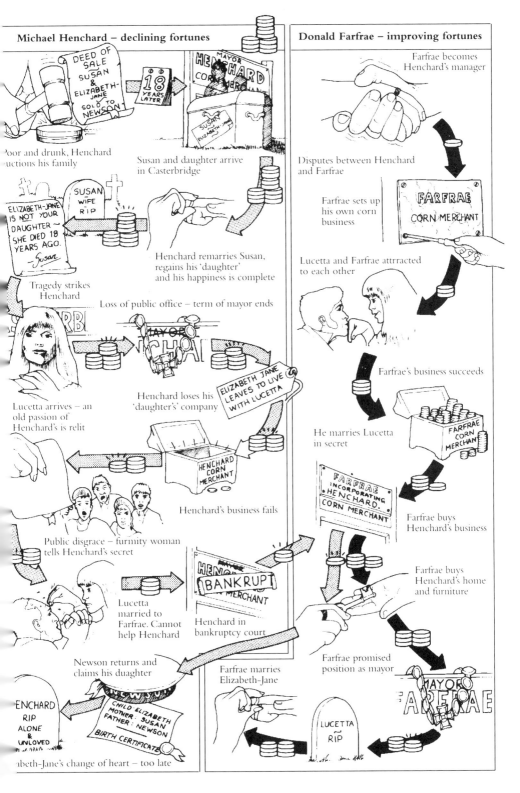

■ Who's who in
The Mayor of Casterbridge

Michael Henchard

As the title of the novel makes clear, Henchard is the tragic hero of the story. He is a heavy-framed man of great physical power. When we meet him at the beginning of the novel he shows a haughty indifference to everyone. The drunken sale of his wife shows that he can be cruel, impulsive and bad-tempered. Henchard's reactions to his deed when he wakes the next day show his repentance, searching for his family for several months. We soon realise that he is a lonely man who has substituted ambition for love.

Henchard is a man with deep, powerful feelings, but who is uneducated and inarticulate. He finds it easier to express his feelings through his actions than through words. Although he is often brutal in his behaviour towards Susan, Elizabeth-Jane and Lucetta, he has a strong sense of responsibility which he shows in his desire to make amends to them.

Unlike the emotionally shallow Farfrae, Henchard learns the need to express love, coming to respect Elizabeth-Jane as a woman, even though she is not his daughter. He also has to learn to accept events beyond his control. He is a victim of fate and has a superstitious nature which often makes him believe there is a sinister power working against him. No sooner does he learn to love Elizabeth-Jane than his love is threatened by the return of Newson. His deception results in her rejection and he dies alone and defeated.

Donald Farfrae

Farfrae is an important character in the novel but his main function is to act as a contrast to Henchard. When he arrives in Casterbridge he is the young, ambitious stranger who is seeking to make his fortune in much the same way as Henchard had done nineteen years earlier. However, we soon see that his character is very much the opposite of Henchard's. He is calculating, moderate and sensible, and easily responds and adapts to the new, scientific farming methods.

Although he sings with great pathos, which endears him to the townsfolk, there seems to be no depth to his emotions. He sacrifices love to ambition in not proposing to Elizabeth-Jane after he has fallen out with Henchard. It is not until after the death of Lucetta that we really see the flaws in his character – although he is fair and generous in his dealings, he fails to feel anything passionately and is more concerned with not making 'a hole in a sovereign'.

Susan Henchard (Newson)

Susan appears at the beginning of the novel to be a meek, even simple-minded woman, but the vehemence with which she throws her wedding ring at Henchard after he has sold her to Newson suggests there is more to her character than meets the eye. Both Henchard and Newson regard her as a simple homespun woman, not at all shrewd or sharp, but she manages to keep Elizabeth-Jane's paternity secret in order to ensure a comfortable future for her, foisting her on Henchard like a cuckoo's egg. But she's also panicked, because someone told her that the 'sale' was not legal and that she is not really married to Newson. She doesn't know her own mind and is essentially a nonentity. The townspeople call her the 'ghost'! She shows cunning in trying to bring Elizabeth-Jane and Farfrae together. Her dedication to her daughter's welfare and future shows her to be both affectionate and self-sacrificing.

Elizabeth-Jane

Elizabeth-Jane is important because, as her character develops, it is through her eyes that we see much of the action: to some extent she replaces the narrator as observer and commentator. She has been taught by poverty and the loss of her father to endure pain and hardship. Although her passage through life is often rough, she endures loneliness and the frustration of her love with quiet patience.

She has natural insight and innate kindness and, even when she loses Farfrae to Lucetta, shows no jealousy. Her strong sense of duty and propriety, however, leads her to reject Henchard at the moment he most needs her love and forgiveness.

The happiness and peace of mind she has found in her marriage to Farfrae is sobered by the bitterness expressed in Henchard's will. She has become, at the end of the novel, a wise and mature woman who regards herself as fortunate, makes the most of limited opportunities, but remains aware of the persistent consequences of unforeseen circumstances.

Lucetta Templeman (La Sueur)

Lucetta is a woman whose past casts a shadow over her life. She is of French descent and comes from Jersey, where she met and cared for Henchard during his illness. They fell in love and their relationship, being contrary to Victorian moral standards, caused a scandal. With the money she inherits from an aunt, she sets herself up in style in Casterbridge.

Her character is shallow, sentimental and artful. She takes great care over her appearance and uses people for her own advantage. Lucetta has a habit of writing letters and, although she fears disclosure of her past, this habit only serves to incriminate her further. Despite having promised to marry Henchard, she refuses to be a slave to the past and secretly marries Farfrae. Ironically, her past is the cause of her death, because the discovery of her letters to Henchard provokes the skimmington ride.

Richard Newson

The character of Newson is not developed and his main function is to help the plot along. He is a kind man and a loving husband and father. His consideration for Susan's feelings, when he knows her to be unhappy about their relationship, makes him go away to sea so that she can return to Henchard if she wishes. His trusting nature borders on the naive and he forgives Henchard's lie, treating it as a practical joke. His love of the sea prevents him from staying long in Casterbridge, even though it means leaving his daughter.

Joshua Jopp

Jopp is a very minor character, but his appearance always appears to signify trouble. In fairness to Jopp, he is a much-abused character. First, he arrives at the corn-factor's office to be told that the position of manager has already been filled. He is bitterly disappointed, and this incident does not endear him to either Farfrae or Henchard. Then he is hired as a manager by Henchard to cut Farfrae out, but when the plan goes wrong, it is Jopp who is blamed and dismissed. Despite Henchard's dislike for the man, he takes lodgings with him. Jopp takes satisfaction from telling Henchard that Farfrae has bought Henchard's house and furniture.

The final rebuff to Jopp is administered by Lucetta when he asks her to speak favourably of him to Farfrae. Armed with Lucetta's package of letters, he enjoys a partial revenge when their contents lead to the skimmington ride, but this ends tragically, leaving Jopp plagued by anxiety. To an extent, his inability to make a real and lasting success of anything he does mirrors the frustrations which afflict Henchard.

Abel Whittle

Abel is one of the rustics and appears at crucial points in the novel. He is unreliable as a workman, being unable to get out of bed in the morning. This brings about the clash between Henchard and Farfrae, when the former treats Abel harshly after he fails to turn up for work on time. The second time we meet Abel is much later in the novel, when Farfrae has taken over Henchard's business. He comments that, though he has to work harder for less money, he is the richer man for enjoying a peace of mind in Farfrae's employ which he never had in Henchard's. Abel performs a simple act of kindness in caring for the dying Henchard at the end of the novel, repaying him for the kindness Henchard showed to Abel's mother.

Themes in
The Mayor of Casterbridge

Setting

Setting

The Mayor of Casterbridge reflects Hardy's intimate knowledge of and interest in the changing face of rural England. That knowledge is evident in his fascinating and detailed accounts of local architecture, references to customs, use of dialect, understanding of economic and social pressures, and sense of history.

In several lyrical passages in the novel, Hardy evokes natural, historic or urban settings which are important backdrops to the intricate web of plot and characterisation. Note, for example, how the historic setting and description of the Ring evoke the gloomiest and most threatening of atmospheres. Whether of the countryside or the urban setting of Casterbridge, detailed descriptions bring both place and people alive.

Casterbridge is portrayed as a town whose existence depends on agriculture. There are no suburbs, and the type of goods in the shops confirms that agriculture pervades business activity. In the centre of town is a busy marketplace, where produce and labour are bought and sold.

During the 19th century, far-reaching changes were occurring in agricultural methods and this too is evident in the novel. In Chapter 1 the turnip-hoer mentions that houses are being pulled down in Weydon-Priors, and Chapter 24 narrates the arrival of the horse-drill in Casterbridge.

Thomas Hardy trained and worked as an architect before concentrating on writing. Consequently there are many detailed descriptions of the architectural features of the buildings of Casterbridge (based on the town of Dorchester). They give a sense of reality to characters and events.

Deception

Deception

The plot hinges on deception of one kind or another. In the first place, Henchard deceives himself that he is making a real effort to trace his wife and child after auctioning them at the fair. Later, Susan deceives Henchard by telling him that Elizabeth-Jane is his daughter. Henchard does not tell Farfrae the whole story of his life and Lucetta holds things back from Elizabeth-Jane and Farfrae. Elizabeth-Jane is deceived by Henchard, Susan and Lucetta.

Perhaps one result of all the deception is the loneliness that seems to afflict many of the characters. Lucetta and Henchard confide in complete strangers on impulse and seem unable to make satisfactory relationships with other people. After her mother's death, Elizabeth-Jane leads a very lonely existence, except for those occasions when she is used by others for their convenience. There is much play with the loneliness of the open road and travellers making their solitary way from place to place.

Structure

Throughout the story there are clues about undercurrents in the plot. For example, the matter of the colour of Elizabeth-Jane's eyes and hair is a clue that all is not as it should be, if she were truly Henchard's daughter. There is the instance of the stranger 'walking the plank' into Casterbridge – is this a hint as to his occupation and therefore his identity?

Many events contrast with and parallel others: the two scenes where Henchard and Farfrae hold sway at the Three Mariners; the two 'rides' which the town turns out to see (the royal procession and the skimmington ride); the fight between two carters which foreshadows that between their masters; the five guineas given to Henchard for Susan which he later returns to her.

It is worth noting that the novel falls into four sections, each shorter than the previous one: Chapters 1–31, 31–40, 41–43 and 44–45. The plot movement in each section is similar. Each section has an initial situation which seems to offer some hope to Henchard, followed by events which create doubt, fear and anxious anticipation for an outcome which results in a catastrophe for him.

■ Text commentary

Chapter 1

A hay-trusser with his wife and child are approaching the village of Weydon-Priors on a late summer's evening. There is a fair in progress and they enter a furmity tent for refreshment. The man takes his furmity laced with rum, and in a drunken state sells his wife and daughter to a sailor for five guineas.

'An atmosphere of stale familiarity'

The opening paragraph presents us with the 'large village of Weydon-Priors' and a young couple so covered in dust as to lend a 'disadvantaged shabbiness' to their appearance. The 'disadvantage' which nature's dust has laid on the couple foreshadows the way in which the whims of nature and fate will affect the pair in the future.

Henchard – dogged and cynical

Henchard is introduced as a fine figure: not a mere labourer, but a 'skilled countryman' carrying the tools of his trade. Note his 'dogged and cynical personal indifference' and remember it as the story unfolds.

The image of a bird, caged or free, appears several times in the story. It reflects the emotions and trials of different characters. Here the 'weak bird' and its 'trite old evening song' echo the tired relationship between the man and woman.

The furmity woman's first appearance

The furmity woman makes four appearances in the novel, linking the changes in Henchard's life. Here, in reasonably respectable and prosperous surroundings, she presides over the momentous events which will set the story's action in motion.

Henchard auctions his wife and child

Henchard complains bitterly about his early marriage, his inability to find work and the thwarting of his ambitions. Notice how the description of the auctioneer selling 'old horses' in the field outside precedes the auction of Susan.

In marked contrast to the normal pattern of an auction, the 'auctioneer', hearing no bids over the initial five shillings, refuses to reduce the price and

16

raises it instead. The sailor, Newson, arrives by chance at the crucial moment. He is a traveller, like so many of the characters – Lucetta, Farfrae, Elizabeth-Jane – whose wanderings reflect the changes taking place in society.

Disgusted at Henchard's behaviour, Susan throws her wedding ring in the hay-trusser's face, symbolising the end of their marriage. She was prepared to stand by her husband, but Henchard, a more volatile character and the weaker for it, succumbs to self-pity.

The auctioned horses lovingly caressing each other contrasts with the Henchards' loveless marriage.

Note that Henchard says he won't go after Susan. There is a pervasive loneliness about Henchard throughout the story. Consider to what extent this loneliness is brought about by his own foolhardiness or by twists of fate.

Chapter 2

When Henchard awakes next morning and remembers what he has done, he makes a hasty departure from the fairground. He swears an oath that he will abstain from liquor for twenty-one years. He searches for his wife and child, finally learning that persons of their description have emigrated.

The morning after...

As Henchard emerges from the tent he surveys a scene marked by ancient remains. Of his own immediate past – his wife and daughter, the furmity woman, the sailor, the auctioneer – there is no sign.

Henchard deeply regrets his actions of the previous night, but although he wishes to find his wife, he also worries about whether he mentioned his name to anybody. It is not clear whether he is more ashamed of his conduct than of people knowing about it. One part of him wants to find his wife and child; another part perhaps enjoys the idea of freedom from responsibilities. He is also 'shy' of revealing the true reasons for his search.

A binding contract?

Susan is described by Henchard as having extreme simplicity of intellect and too much meekness. This perhaps explains why she believes there is some binding force in the auction. However, one shouldn't dismiss Susan's intellect too quickly. Later she has the presence of mind to keep her daughter's true parentage secret in the hope that she might gain some advantage for her. Susan also writes the anonymous notes that bring Elizabeth-Jane and Farfrae together later in the novel.

A promise made

Setting

Filled with remorse at his actions, Henchard takes an oath to avoid strong liquor. For this he requires a 'fit place and imagery', revealing his superstitious nature. His oath is no light promise to be broken at the first opportunity. He means what he says. Elizabeth-Jane recognises this trait in Henchard when, at the end of the novel, she fulfils the conditions of his will.

Chapter 3

Nineteen years later, Susan Henchard and her daughter, Elizabeth-Jane, are approaching Weydon-Priors by the same road on fair day. Susan now calls herself Mrs Newson. The two women are in mourning for the sailor, Richard Newson. The fair is smaller, but the furmity woman is still there, though fallen on hard times. Susan learns from her that Henchard was in Casterbridge twelve months after selling his wife.

Susan and Elizabeth-Jane return

The arrival of Susan and Elizabeth-Jane at Weydon-Priors contrasts with their arrival there, with Henchard, nineteen years earlier. They walk hand-in-hand and demonstrate simple affection for each other. Henchard will pass this way again at the end of the novel, but with no one to comfort his loneliness.

The symbol of lonely figures on an open road recurs in the novel. Be aware of how frequently characters walk alone to accidental or arranged meetings which will lead to momentous changes in their lives.

Hardy emphasises the passing of time by noting the many social changes occurring in rural areas. Business at Weydon Fair has dwindled, and there is evidence of the advance of 'civilisation' and the disruption of the rural way of life. Some of the fair's roundabouts show signs of mechanisation.

Deception

Susan is trying to find Henchard now that the sailor Newson has been lost at sea. She has not told Elizabeth-Jane about her relationship to Henchard, thus beginning the various deceptions, tragedies, and misunderstandings in the novel.

The observation of the furmity woman that ''tis the sly and underhand that get on in these times' is a curiously ironic, though not strictly accurate comment on some of the deceptions that take place in this story. When questioned, the old furmity seller has difficulty recalling the sale of a wife. Ironically, a few years later she demonstrates how well she is able to remember the incident.

Respectable Elizabeth-Jane

Elizabeth-Jane has a highly developed sense of what she considers to be respectable. Although not actually related to Henchard by blood, she shows some of the same ambition to improve her lot which is such a driving force in him. Equally, we can see in her the result of Susan's dedicated desire to improve the lot of her daughter, even if it means misleading Henchard into accepting her as his own child.

Chapter 4

An outline of Susan's life with Newson, first in Canada and then in Falmouth, is given as a flashback. A friend of Susan ridicules her belief that there is anything legally binding in her relationship with Newson. Shortly after, Newson is reported lost at sea. Susan sets out to try to find a better life for Elizabeth-Jane by searching for her husband, Michael Henchard. They arrive in Casterbridge where the people are up in arms against the corn-factor who has sold overgrown wheat, making the bread indigestible.

Susan – a simple person?

The author comments on the simplicity of Susan's belief that Newson had acquired a 'morally real and justifiable right to her'. It helps to explain why she stayed with him.

Newson shows sensitivity towards Susan's feelings. He recognises her recent disillusionment at their relationship and immediately resolves to free her. Notice how, later, he shows understanding of Henchard's predicament when Newson himself suddenly arrives in search of Elizabeth-Jane.

Susan has suffered personally, but what drives her on is a desire to assist 'the young mind of her companion (which) was struggling for enlargement'. At the same time, Elizabeth-Jane 'sought further into things than other girls in her position ever did'.

Susan felt she had to return to Henchard once she was aware of the real bond between Newson and herself.

Susan's reluctance to make too hasty an enquiry after Henchard reinforces our awareness of her real reasons for wishing to find her husband – and it has nothing to do with love! She and Elizabeth-Jane hear Henchard's name and then hear about a corn-factor who has sold grown wheat to the bakers. Although the two are not yet linked, suspicion is created in our minds that they might be related.

Rural change

Hardy gives a detailed description of Casterbridge, conveying the agricultural and pastoral character of the town and people. The description of the trades carried on in Casterbridge indicates how much it depends on the countryside for its very survival.

Setting

Chapter 5

The two women proceed to the King's Arms where they observe Henchard, now Mayor of Casterbridge and successful corn merchant. The loftiness of his social position makes Susan nervous about approaching him. They notice that Henchard drinks water, though wine and rum are available.

Descriptive devices, clothing and rustics

A common descriptive device used by Hardy is the framing of a scene through a window or doorway. Look for other examples of this and see how it links events on either side of the 'framing'. Also be aware of detailed descriptions of clothing. Clothing defines social position: here, for example, it helps to contrast Henchard the successful mayor with the skilled countryman of Susan's memory.

Setting

The rustics of Casterbridge add humour to the narrative. They also comment on the behaviour of their 'betters', and – as in the skimmington ride and the conflicting celebrations put on by Henchard and Farfrae later in the novel – are active in moving the narrative along.

Susan hesitates. Who is Elizabeth Jane?

If Susan has searched for Henchard in order to secure a future for Elizabeth-Jane, why is she intimidated by finding him so successful? Could it be that she fears his success may put him beyond the half-laid plans she has made?

Nineteen years have passed since the wife-sale. The oath has two years to run, yet in Chapter 3 Hardy describes Elizabeth-Jane as a young woman of about eighteen. Does this discrepancy have any significance? There is a variety of clues as to the true identity of Elizabeth-Jane: descriptions of her eyes, and references to 'her' rather than 'their' daughter when speaking of Susan and Henchard, are two examples.

■ Self-test (Questions) Chapters 1–5

Uncover the plot

Delete two of the three alternatives given, to find the correct plot. Beware possible misconceptions and muddles.

Michael Henchard arrives at the Fair at Weydon Priors with his wife and child, where he gets drunk and sells them both for five pounds/guineas/shillings. Repenting the next morning, he vows not to touch women/money/alcohol for a week/the next twenty-one years/the rest of his life, and sets out to find them. Failing, he travels to Casterbridge/goes to sea/dies. Years later, on the death of her 'purchaser' Newson, Susan hopes to sell/advance/enlighten her now grown-up daughter, who does not know who her true father is. The two seek out Henchard at Casterbridge, where he has become the wealthy and popular/unscrupulous/friendly Mayor.

Who? What? Why? When? Where? How?

1 What is Henchard's trade?
2 Why has the family travelled to Weydon Priors?
3 What does Henchard say Susan 'had no business to take'?
4 Why does Henchard stop looking for his wife and child?
5 Where does Susan first become aware that her 'situation' is improper, and how does her 'enlightenment' come about?
6 How does Susan explain her search for Henchard to Elizabeth-Jane?
7 What is the general 'shape' of Casterbridge?
8 Who has supplied the bad corn to the millers and bakers?
9 When does Solomon Longways say Henchard will be able to drink alcohol again?
10 When does Henchard say he will take back the 'growed wheat', and what is the implication of this?

Who is this?

From your knowledge of the characters in the novel, identify the following people.

1 'The man was of fine figure, swarthy, and stern in aspect.'
2 Who said kindly: 'the little one too – the more the merrier!'?
3 '...her freedom from levity of character and the extreme simplicity of her intellect.'
4 'They walked with joined hands... the act of simple affection.'
5 'The desire – sober and repressed – of (her) heart was to see, to hear, and to understand.'

Familiar themes

In these opening chapters Hardy introduces several important themes and images. Look at the following lines, and decide if they illustrate youth/age, change/continuity, social divisions, fate/irony, or 'the theatre' – or a combination of these.

1 'To watch, it was like looking at some grand feat of stagery from a darkened auditorium.'
2 'While life's middle summer had set its hardening mark on the mother's face, her former spring-like specialities were transferred so dexterously by Time to... her child.'
3 'The new periodical great markets of neighbouring towns were beginning to interfere seriously with the trade carried on here for centuries.'
4 'As we plainer fellows bain't invited, they leave the winder-shutters open that we may get jist a sense o't out here.'
5 '... she had replied that she would not hear him say that many times before it happened, in the resigned tones of a fatalist.'

Open quotes

Complete the following useful quotes. The numbers in brackets refer to the chapters in which they can be found.

1 'Tis like Susan to show some idiotic simplicity. Meek – ...' (2)
2 'When Newson came home at the end of one winter he saw that...' (4)
3 'How could she become a woman of wider knowledge...' (4)
4 '... this antiquated borough, the borough of Casterbridge...' (4)
5 '(That laugh) fell in well with conjectures of a temperament which would have no pity for weakness...' (5)

Self-test (Answers) Chapters 1–5

Uncover the plot

Michael Henchard arrives at the Fair at Weydon Priors with his wife and child, where he gets drunk and sells them both for five guineas. Repenting the next morning, he vows not to touch alcohol for the next twenty-one years, and sets out to find them. Failing, he travels to Casterbridge. Years later, on the death of her 'purchaser' Newson, Susan hopes to advance her now grown-up daughter, who does not know who her true father is. The two seek out Henchard at Casterbridge, where he has become the unscrupulous Mayor.

Who? What? Why? When? Where? How?

1 Hay-trusser (1)
2 To find work (and accommodation) (1)
3 The child (1)
4 When he hears that persons answering to his description have emigrated (2)
5 At Falmouth; a friend ridicules her acceptance of the situation (4)
6 Looking for a relation by marriage (3)
7 Square (4)
8 Henchard (4, 5)
9 In two years' time (5)
10 When he can turn the bad wheat into good; he believes this is impossible, so it is implied that he does not intend to compensate the millers/bakers (5)

Who is this?

1 Henchard (1)
2 Newson (1)
3 Susan (2)
4 Susan and Elizabeth-Jane (3)
5 Elizabeth-Jane (4)

Familiar themes

1 The theatre (1)
2 Youth/age; continuity (3)
3 Change (3)
4 Social divisions (5)
5 Fate/irony (2)

Open quotes

1 '...that meekness has done me more harm than the bitterest temper!' (2)
2 '...the delusion he had so carefully sustained had vanished for ever.' (4)
3 '...higher repute – 'better', as she termed it – this was her constant inquiry of her mother.' (4)
4 '...at that time, recent as it was, untouched by the faintest sprinkle of modernism.' (4)
5 '...but would be ready to yield ungrudging admiration to greatness, and strength.' (5)

Chapter 6

At the King's Arms, a young man called Donald Farfrae overhears the criticisms levelled at the corn-factor and sends a note to him. He then decides to lodge at the more modest Three Mariners inn. Susan and Elizabeth-Jane also decide to stay there. Later in the evening, Henchard goes to see Farfrae at the inn.

A stranger arrives

Again a stranger enters Henchard's life. Like the sailor Newson, he is a traveller. Our first impression of Farfrae is of a young man of 'pleasant aspect'.

Note how the main characters are drawn together here: Elizabeth-Jane and Susan are drawn to the mayor because of their 'relationship', whilst Farfrae is drawn to assist a man who is in trouble through no great fault of his own. At the same time, Farfrae brings himself to Elizabeth-Jane's notice and, by asking about a hotel, ensures that they all end up staying at the same place.

Important letters

Letters are used to give shape and continuity to the plot. This note from Farfrae to Henchard results in Farfrae abandoning his voyage to America and staying on in Casterbridge as Henchard's manager. There will be other occasions where letters or notes are central to the action: Susan's note, intended to bring Farfrae and Elizabeth-Jane together; Lucetta's letters to Henchard which she wishes returned; Susan's letter to Henchard disclosing Elizabeth-Jane's parentage; and Henchard's last instructions on his deathbed. There are others – look out for them as you read the novel.

Chapter 7

Elizabeth-Jane works in the Three Mariners to pay for the lodgings. Susan overhears Farfrae telling Henchard how to restore the grown wheat. The corn-factor is so grateful to the young man that he offers him a job as his manager. Farfrae declines, as he has made up his mind to go to America. Before he leaves, Henchard declines a drink, explaining that he swore an oath against strong liquor out of shame for a past deed.

Paying their way

Susan's practical approach to respectability – 'We must pay our way' – is in total contrast to her daughter's attitude. Elizabeth-Jane is described as a person of innate kindness, willing to make self-sacrifices. Look for more evidence of this as the novel progresses. There is an ironic twist to her offer to help serve dinner at the inn. The respectability which she craves is sacrificed to her willingness to help out in the inn so as to reduce their bill. This same act will later rouse Henchard's wrath and drive him to doubt her 'respectability'.

A manager for Henchard, and a guilty conscience

The coincidence of the ladies being in the room next to Farfrae's enables us to hear the conversation between the two men. Henchard has assumed that Farfrae was the man who had applied for the job as his manager. The chance arrival of Farfrae in Casterbridge at just the moment when Henchard was looking for a manager, and his obvious ability to fulfil the position, provide the impetus for the plot to develop.

Note the conversation between the two men: the way in which Henchard tries to play down his interest in Farfrae's invention, and Farfrae's openness: he could easily have charged a high premium for the information he gives to Henchard.

Henchard offers Farfrae a job as manager of the corn business. His plea to Farfrae to stay is ironic in the light of later events, as the Scot will one day replace him as corn-factor and mayor.

> Note the irony here. Henchard previously gave all he had to a stranger in return for five guineas. In return for another 'bargain', he again puts all his worldly goods at the disposal of another stranger.
>
> We discover that, although Henchard has been successful and has proved his strength by shouldering his responsibilities and sticking to his oath, he is still plagued by guilt.

Chapter 8

The Scotsman, Farfrae, joins the assembled company at the Three Mariners and gives a recital of some of his native songs. Everyone is very impressed by the feeling he shows, particularly Elizabeth-Jane. Henchard, in the street outside, also hears Farfrae's voice and is drawn to him.

Farfrae performs

Farfrae sings with great effect, winning the hearts of the whole company at the Three Mariners. Farfrae's openness with Henchard and the ease with which he makes friends predispose us to like him.

The 'framing' device is used here by means of the heart-shaped holes through which Henchard hears the Scot's song. They symbolise not only the attraction which Henchard feels towards Farfrae, but also his separation. There is a stark contrast here between the lonely Henchard on one side of the shutter and the convivial Farfrae on the other.

Chapter 9

Next morning, Henchard accompanies Farfrae to the Bristol road. Susan sends Elizabeth-Jane to Henchard with a letter. When she arrives, she finds Farfrae there instead of Henchard. We discover that Farfrae has been persuaded to stay on in Casterbridge.

The scene is now set for a number of new developments in the plot. September in Weydon-Priors, during which Henchard held centre-stage for a short while and split his family, has given way to September in Casterbridge nineteen years later, where he again holds centre-stage, this time as mayor.

Henchard wishes Farfrae well

It is ironic that Henchard should wish Farfrae well, and declare how he 'shall often think' of the help he received from him. It will not be long before Henchard will regret this, and later he will find himself the recipient of further help from Farfrae when their roles are reversed

Notice Henchard's impulsive nature: 'Now you are my friend!' After only a short acquaintance, Henchard has given Farfrae responsibility for his corn business, taken him into his own home, and elevated him almost to the position of a lifelong friend and confidant. However, you should note that at no time in the novel does Farfrae abuse Henchard's trust.

Chapter 10

Before Elizabeth-Jane can enter Henchard's office, Joshua Jopp pushes in and announces himself as the new manager. He is disappointed to learn that the position has been filled. Elizabeth-Jane gives Susan's letter to Henchard, who sends her back with a letter for Susan, in which he encloses five guineas. He arranges to meet Susan at the Ring on the Budmouth road.

Visitors from the past

Note the biblical allusion to the 'quicker cripple at Bathesda' which Hardy uses to illustrate and comment on Joshua Jopp's entry to the corn-factor's office. In the Bible, the first cripple into the pool at Bethesda, after it had been disturbed by an angel, was cured. Jopp is obviously anxious to lay claim to 'his' job when he steps past Elizabeth-Jane into Henchard's office.

Henchard's treatment of Joshua Jopp is hardly justified. It throws some light on his attitude to running a business and gives an insight into his nature. Henchard is not a man of soft words or indecisive action.

Henchard's first emotions on hearing the news of Susan's reappearance with a daughter are relief and gratitude that Susan has not made his actions widely known, or told

Elizabeth-Jane. This shows that he still feels guilty for his actions, nineteen years after the auction took place.

Elizabeth-Jane is surprised at the 'gentle delicacy' of Henchard's manner, which contrasts strongly with his brusque and unmannerly treatment of Jopp. His dining-room reflects his physical appearance, with its heavy mahogany furniture which has legs 'shaped like those of an elephant' and the huge folio volumes of religious works.

Henchard's guilty conscience is at work when he gives Elizabeth-Jane five pounds enclosed with the note to Susan. The five shillings which he adds as an afterthought makes the sum up to five guineas – the amount he received for the sale of Susan and his daughter – a gesture to Susan which indicates his awareness of the wrong he has done her.

Note the oddity of his next thought – to ask himself suddenly if the two women might not be imposters – particularly odd in the light of his unquestioning acceptance of the new arrival Farfrae into his life. What is so ironic, though, is that Elizabeth-Jane *is* an imposter, though only Susan knows this at present. To compound the irony, he finds 'a something in Elizabeth-Jane (which) soon assured him' that she is his daughter.

Henchard's cup overflows

Henchard's interest in Farfrae is eclipsed by the arrival of Susan and Elizabeth-Jane. He has gained, within the space of a day, a new manager, a returning wife, and a grown daughter. Small wonder that he remarks: 'It never rains but it pours!' – yet is this an appropriate response to the overwhelming blessings that appear to be descending upon him, or is it more like prophetic irony?

Chapter 11

An atmosphere of gloom is created by the Ring with its gruesome historical associations. Henchard meets Susan and proposes a plan whereby he can court and remarry her without revealing his past, either publicly or to Elizabeth-Jane.

Skeletons from the past

The novel is placed in historical perspective by reference to Roman remains.

Setting

Note the gloomy yet strangely relevant detail that speaks of skeletons being dug up in and around Casterbridge. The 'skeleton' from Henchard's past is about to rise up and confront him. The 'Melancholy, impressive, lonely' nature of the spot reflects the significance of this meeting between Susan and Henchard. One kind of appointment seldom had a place there – 'that of happy lovers'.

The details of the description of this first meeting – the absence of the need for speech, Henchard supporting Susan in his arms, his first words telling of his abstinence from drink, her head bowed in unspoken acknowledgement and acceptance of his admission and repentance – all speak of reconciliation, understanding and love. But we are soon

Deception to see the relevance of Hardy's description of the Ring as a place where no happy lovers meet and where intrigues take place. Both Susan and Henchard agree to deceive Elizabeth-Jane about her parenthood, but Susan's is a double deceit which involves her in continuing her deception of Henchard.

Henchard has secrets to keep

There is a comment later in the novel to the effect that if Henchard's past sins had become public knowledge sooner, it is likely that his fellow townsfolk would have looked upon them as the excesses of youth and dismissed them. But now his attempts to keep them hidden, which began in Chapter 2 with his concern about whether he had disclosed his name in the furmity tent, are about to catch up with him.

A binding agreement

Susan believed that, although she was not legally married to Newson, there was something solemn and binding in the bargain. The fact that Newson had paid for her in good faith was enough to make her believe that she owed him fidelity.

Note how Susan confirms the main motive behind her desire to return to Henchard – the welfare of Elizabeth-Jane. She says that she would be content 'for herself' to leave immediately and never bother Henchard again.

> Has Susan forgiven her husband? Her response leaves the matter in some doubt, as indeed there would seem to be some doubt about whether Henchard really loves her. Certainly their parting exchange seems to bear out Hardy's statement that lovers rarely meet at the Ring.

Chapter 12

Returning home from his meeting with Susan, Henchard invites Farfrae to supper and confides in him the story of his marriage and separation from Susan. He tells him of his plans to remarry her and the complication posed by a woman in Jersey whom he has also offered to marry. He asks Farfrae to help him draft a letter explaining the circumstances which prevent him from fulfilling his promise. He does not tell Farfrae that he sold his wife and daughter.

Farfrae takes over

Donald Farfrae

Farfrae shows great skill at sorting out the corn-factor's paperwork. Henchard is 'mentally and physically unfit' for such work. Note the striking contrast between their respective attitudes to the business. Henchard is a traditional rustic businessman working by rule-of-thumb and instinct. Farfrae is a representative of modern business methods. He also shows sensitivity in recognising the strengths and weaknesses in Henchard's character.

Henchard's loneliness

Henchard returns to the topic of his loneliness. Success in business and his position as Mayor of Casterbridge do nothing to alleviate that loneliness and may, indeed, be among its causes. He confides his problems to Farfrae scarcely a day after meeting him for the first time. He has gone through considerable emotional turmoil in the last day or so, and needs to confide in someone.

Michael Henchard

We suddenly learn something new about Henchard's past, and how he feels that 'by doing right by Susan I wrong another innocent woman'. Henchard shows his willingness to accept responsibility for his past in wishing to make amends to both Susan and Lucetta. Note how he draws Farfrae even more closely into his personal affairs by asking him to write the letter to the 'young lady' in Jersey.

More deceit

Farfrae's advice to tell the truth is rejected by Henchard. Also, instead of taking Elizabeth-Jane into their confidence, Henchard and Susan play an elaborate charade of courtship – 'to keep our child's respect', – the very thing that Henchard will eventually lose.

Deception

Henchard's doubts and musings as he returns from posting his letter are shortly to receive their answer. Note the irony here: he disposed of Susan for five guineas, but she returned to him. He now hopes to dispose of the other woman in his life, also with a payment. Later he will be desperate for Lucetta to act as his guarantor.

Self-test (Questions) Chapters 6–12

Uncover the plot

Delete two of the three alternatives given, to find the correct plot. Beware possible misconceptions and muddles.

Elizabeth-Jane and her mother stay at a cottage/the King's Arms/the Three Mariners and overhear a conversation between Henchard and Joshua Jopp/Christopher Coney/Donald Farfrae, a young traveller who shows Henchard how to restore corn. Henchard invites him to become his manager/musician/hay-trusser; eventually he accepts. Elizabeth-Jane visits the Mayor at his house with a message from her mother; he agrees to meet Elizabeth-Jane/Susan/Mother Cuxsom at the Ring, and they plan to live together again without telling their daughter the true situation. Henchard confides in Farfrae, revealing that he is a drunkard/a womaniser/engaged to another woman. Believing his first duty to be his job/Elizabeth-Jane/Susan, he breaks off the engagement.

Who? What? Why? When? How?

1 Who is 'ruddy and of a fair countenance, bright-eyed, and slight in build'?
2 What is 'the common weal'?
3 Who is Joshua Jopp?
4 What moves Farfrae about Henchard?
5 How do the townsfolk react to Farfrae's singing?
6 How does Buzzford describe Casterbridge?
7 Who does Elizabeth-Jane admire, and why?
8 What are Henchard's first words to Susan?
9 What is the plan of Henchard and his wife?
10 What is Farfrae's advice to the Mayor?

Who is this?

From your knowledge of the characters in the novel, identify the following people.
1 Who notices, and of whom: 'how his cheek was so truly curved as to be part of a globe'?
2 Who is characterised by 'a willingness to sacrifice her personal comfort and dignity to the common weal'?
3 Who thinks, of whom, that 'his employer was a man who knew no moderation in his requests and impulses'?
4 Who has 'the marks of introspective inflexibility' on his features?
5 Who is 'the poor forgiving woman'?

Familiar themes

Temperance/balance/sobriety of lifestyle, temper and behaviour is a strong theme in the novel. Identify the following lines/passages, giving chapter numbers, and say what kind of temperance or intemperance is being explored.
1 'Men were putting their heads together in twos and threes, telling good stories, with pantomimic laughter which reached convulsive grimace.'
2 'She was a girl characterised by earnestness and soberness of mien, with which simple drapery accorded well.'
3 'In addition to these fixed obstacles which spoke so cheerfully of individual unrestraint as to boundaries...'
4 'I am the most distant fellow in the world when I don't care for a man... but when a man takes my fancy he takes it strong.'
5 '...philandering with womankind has neither been my vice nor my virtue.'

Prove it!

Find a quote from the text that could be used to back up each of the following statements.
1 Henchard regrets his past action with regards his wife and daughter.
2 Elizabeth-Jane and Farfrae have much in common.
3 Casterbridge is not separate from the country.
4 Susan acts for Elizabeth-Jane and not herself.
5 Henchard intends to do well by Susan and Elizabeth-Jane.

■ Self-test (Answers) Chapters 6–12

Uncover the plot

Elizabeth-Jane and her mother stay at the Three Mariners and overhear a conversation between Henchard and Donald Farfrae, a young traveller who shows Henchard how to restore corn. Henchard invites him to become his manager; eventually he accepts. Elizabeth-Jane visits the Mayor at his house with a message from her mother; he agrees to meet Susan at the Ring, and they plan to live together again without telling their daughter the true situation. Henchard confides in Farfrae, revealing that he is engaged to another woman. Believing his first duty to be to Susan, he breaks off the engagement.

Who? What? Why? When? How?

1 Donald Farfrae (6)
2 The general good (7)
3 The man originally intended to be Henchard's manager (7)
4 His 'warm convictions of (Farfrae's) value' (7)
5 Attentive, moved (8)
6 '... a old, hoary place o' wickedness' (8)
7 Farfrae, for 'the serious light in which he looked at serious things' (8)
8 'I don't drink' (11)
9 For Susan and her daughter to take a cottage in the name of Newson; for Henchard to court and marry Susan; for Elizabeth-Jane to remain in ignorance of the past (11)
10 To tell Elizabeth-Jane the truth (12)

Who is this?

1 Elizabeth-Jane of Farfrae (7)
2 Elizabeth-Jane (7)
3 Farfrae, of Henchard (12)
4 Henchard (12)
5 Susan (9)

Familiar themes

1 Chapter 6; drunkenness, overeating
2 Chapter 8; dignity in sobriety of dress and manner
3 Chapter 9; a lack of architectural restraint
4 Chapter 9; extremes of character
5 Chapter 12; the potential ill-effects of loose living

Prove it!

1 'I did a deed on account of it which I shall be ashamed of to my dying day.' (7)
2 'It was extraordinary how similar their views were.' (8)
3 'Casterbridge was the complement of the rural life around; not its urban opposite.' (9)
4 'I came here for the sake of Elizabeth...' (11)
5 'Judge me by my future works...' (11)

Chapter 13

Henchard hires a cottage for Susan and Elizabeth-Jane where he visits them frequently. After a few months he marries Susan and, although it is not a joyous occasion, the plan is almost complete. Henchard has fulfilled his three resolves, namely to make amends to Susan, to provide a home for Elizabeth-Jane and to punish himself for his past sins.

Setting

The mood is set by a description of the autumnal evening sun and of the historical remains surrounding the cottage which Henchard has rented for Susan. 'The usual touch of melancholy that a past-marked prospect lends' appropriately describes the cottage in view of what happens later, when the past revisits the inhabitants.

The casual conversations Henchard has with Susan, intended to avoid seeming too familiar in front of Elizabeth-Jane, amuse Henchard. We are reminded of his laugh, which was described as 'not encouraging to strangers' in Chapter 5. Certainly Susan does not find the situation amusing. Note also the description of his actions as the 'course of strict mechanical rightness...at any expense to the later one (the woman from Jersey) and to his own sentiments'. It confirms that, at this moment, he is acting purely out of duty, though he does eventually come to love Elizabeth-Jane.

Susan is worried about their deception of Elizabeth-Jane. But she is more afraid of having to reveal the past to her daughter. Note also the reference to 'her' girl's reputation. She knows that Henchard has no part in Elizabeth-Jane.

Deception

Henchard's day of happiness

The marriage of Henchard and Susan is not an exciting event and the mood is conveyed by the description of the weather.

Note the prophetic irony of Henchard's remark that he will soon be able to leave everything to Farfrae and that he will have more time to call his own. Eventually Farfrae will own Henchard's business, his house, his furniture, and will marry his 'daughter'.

Although Henchard wants to make amends to Susan and provide a home for Elizabeth-Jane, his third resolve is to punish himself and, although he gives no clear idea how this will be done, it is possible that the marriage itself and all its responsibilities is his idea of punishment. Certainly he does not seem to have much love for Susan.

Chapter 14

Susan and Elizabeth-Jane now lead easier and more affluent lives. Elizabeth-Jane continues to dress modestly and does not draw attention to herself by spending a lot of money. Susan opposes the final part of Henchard's plan to adopt her daughter and change her name. Someone plays a trick on Elizabeth-Jane and Farfrae by arranging for them to meet at an empty granary.

Happiness passes Henchard by

Michael Henchard

Henchard shows as much kindness to Susan 'as a man, mayor and churchwarden could' – but what about as a husband and lover? He finds it impossible to love her since, in a perverse way, he still blames her for going off with Newson and for demeaning his present dignity.

Elizabeth-Jane takes care

Elizabeth-Jane

The relatively affluent life which Elizabeth-Jane is now able to live makes it possible for her to develop. Nonetheless, ever-mindful of the poverty she and her mother have suffered before, she is very careful in the way she dresses, resisting the temptation to buy anything which isn't strictly necessary.

Mysteries and deceits

The deceptions which are so frequent in this story are brought to mind again

Deception

by Henchard's noticing the changed colour of Elizabeth-Jane's hair. Note Susan's discomfort at his query – 'to which future held the key'.

The mystery surrounding Elizabeth-Jane is compounded by Susan's reaction to Henchard's suggestion that Elizabeth-Jane's surname should be changed to Henchard. Why should she object to such a change? Note also the clever way she prevails upon her daughter to reject the suggestion. Susan is certainly not just a simple, meek nonentity.

Henchard's affection for Farfrae

Farfrae's innovations in managing the corn trade enable it to thrive, but 'the rugged picturesqueness of the old method disappears with its inconveniences'. Although Henchard has little respect for Farfrae's physical strength, he shows admiration for his intellectual abilities. Note the prophetic description of Henchard being supported by Farfrae's slight figure.

> Further insights into Henchard's character and much of the following action are given through the discerning eye of Elizabeth-Jane. Hardy identifies her with the view of the narrator. It is through Elizabeth-Jane's natural insight that we see Henchard's affection for Farfrae, his tendency to domineer and the first suggestion of a possible rift between the two men in the future.

A practical joke

Elizabeth-Jane and Farfrae meet at the Durnover Hill granary, having both

received similar notes. Given the affection which Henchard has for both of them, it is reasonable to suppose that it is he who should try to bring them together – but in fact it is Susan who has written the notes.

Examine the reactions of these two people to their meeting. Were they really as calm as their conversation suggests? What would be the likely effect on each of them of Farfrae delicately blowing dust and husks off 'her back hair, and her side hair, and her neck, and the crown of her bonnet, and the fur of her victorine', and of Elizabeth-Jane saying 'O, thank you,' at every puff? Farfrae seems very thoughtful as she leaves!

Chapter 15

Elizabeth-Jane is admired in the town for her beauty and dress sense. A rift appears in the friendship of Henchard and Farfrae when they quarrel over Henchard's treatment of one of his workmen. Henchard comes off worse, finding he has lost some of the respect he had among the townsfolk. Their friendship continues, but Henchard often wishes that he had not confided the secrets of his past to Farfrae.

Elizabeth-Jane begins to 'find herself'

Elizabeth-Jane discovers she is attractive to others. Her new clothes bring her the admiration of the townsfolk but, ironically, she is afraid of posing as someone she is not.

Abel Whittle's breeches

The argument over Henchard's treatment of Abel Whittle reveals a sharp contrast between the characters of Henchard and Farfrae. Henchard takes no account of the man's feelings: Farfrae is sensitive to them. However, later on, Farfrae later makes his own employees work harder for less money. It would be too easy to suggest that Henchard's treatment of Abel Whittle shows him to be totally unjust and unfeeling. If he were such a man, he would not have kept Abel's mother in coals and snuff all the previous winter.

Henchard is uneasy about Farfrae

Henchard's conversation with a child, sent to fetch Farfrae, unsettles him. He has been used to being the man of position, wealth and authority, respected and feared by all. Suddenly his position begins to be put in question, in the townspeople's eyes, by Farfrae. Henchard regrets having revealed the secrets of his past to Farfrae and starts to think of him with a 'dim dread'. His fears are not justified, because Farfrae will not act directly against him except in fair competition later. Farfrae never bears Henchard any malice.

Chapter 16

On the occasion of a national holiday, both men organise separate festivities. Henchard's are elaborate, in the open air and free of charge. Farfrae's are under cover and a charge is made for admission. On the day, it rains heavily and Henchard's festivities are washed out. Farfrae's are successful and the comments of the townsfolk goad Henchard into saying that his manager is about to leave him. Farfrae takes him at his word.

Rival entertainments

Although the rift between Henchard and Farfrae is largely a result of Henchard's actions, fate intervenes in the form of bad weather, making a complete fiasco of his entertainments. Perhaps it isn't only the bad weather that prevented the townspeople from coming, maybe they are beginning to feel an attraction to Farfrae. The rival entertainments foreshadow the later rivalry of Henchard and Farfrae in business and personal affairs.

Henchard walks in the shadows of Farfrae's celebrations. Again he is the outsider, looking in on Farfrae's social success.

Henchard regrets a decision

At the beginning of the story, Henchard, drunk and sorry for himself 'dismissed' his wife and child from his life. They have returned and set in train events that will prove catastrophic for him. Now, 'drunk' with jealousy and self-pity, he dismisses Farfrae. Note how the next morning, as before, he regrets the actions of the previous night.

Chapter 17

After the festivities, Farfrae walks Elizabeth-Jane home and almost proposes to her. When he leaves Henchard's employment, he sets up in business on his own, at first avoiding competition with him, but later having to engage in commercial competition in defence of his business. Henchard forbids Farfrae to see Elizabeth-Jane.

A love match?

Elizabeth-Jane realises she is in love with Farfrae but, although he comes close to proposing to her, he decides that the time is not suitable. His actions suggest his calculating nature. His judgement of what is right in relation to his dealings with other people needs to be looked at carefully, especially where his personal feelings are involved.

Henchard begins to isolate himself

Henchard's jealousy, impulsiveness and ill-temper, which have caused the rift with his friend and manager, now isolate him from the community which does not share his feelings of enmity towards Farfrae. Not content with that, he now presses Elizabeth-Jane to reject Farfrae. Henchard sends a note to Farfrae requesting that he does not attempt to see Elizabeth-Jane again. Ironically, as Hardy points out, if Henchard were to encourage him to be his son-in-law, it could possibly heal the rift between them. Susan, despite her concern for her daughter, has no part to play in this affair.

Note the physical imagery involved in describing the commercial conflict between Henchard and Farfrae. Later, the two men actually fight and Henchard wins in the physical sense, but Farfrae 'wins' morally.

To emphasise Henchard's isolation, Hardy refers to the mythical hero Bellerophon who, deserted by the gods, wandered alone, facing many hazardous tasks.

Chapter 18

A letter arrives from Jersey. A young woman, Lucetta, writes to Henchard and asks him to return her old letters when she passes through Casterbridge. She fails to keep the appointment and Henchard is left with the packet of letters. Susan falls ill and writes a letter to her husband with the instructions that it should not be opened until Elizabeth-Jane's wedding day. Susan confesses to having written the notes which brought her daughter and Farfrae together at the granary, then dies.

> Conveniently, Susan is about to die as Lucetta is brought to the fore. This sequence of events opens the way to more conflict in the relationships between Elizabeth-Jane, Lucetta, Farfrae and Henchard.

'Past-marked prospects'

Setting

As Henchard reads the letter from Lucetta, the phrase 'a vista of past enactments' echoes the 'past-marked prospects' (Ch 13). The integration of past history and present events is a continuing theme, exemplified in the ever-present embodiments of the past in ancient barrows and other remains; the ever-present reminder of Henchard's past in Susan and Elizabeth-Jane; and now Lucetta, another figure from his past, returning to haunt him.

Deception

In her note, Lucetta forgives Henchard for the dilemma he has placed her in and requests the return of certain letters. She acknowledges that there was no deceit on his part regarding Susan's return and that the only course open to him was to re-marry Susan. Perhaps the only time that Henchard has been totally free of deceit, when it mattered, was when he took Farfrae's advice about what to say in his letter to Lucetta!

Henchard considers how he 'ought' to marry Lucetta if the opportunity arises. Note how there is no element of desire, passion, or love in the conclusion he reaches.

Letters and notes

Susan's letter will be opened at the wrong time by Henchard. Lucetta's letters will also be opened at the wrong time and by the wrong man later in the novel – both events have tragic consequences.

Susan Henchard

The death of Susan

Susan, like Henchard, is a superstitious person. Four pennies are to be used as weights to close her eyes after she has died. The superstitious belief was that if a person's eyes remained open they became a ghost.

Note the irony of 'her wishes and ways will all be as nothing!' Despite the fact that she is the least forceful of the main characters, Susan's two main desires are fulfilled: she brings her daughter into the safekeeping of Henchard's house and, although she does not live to see it, Elizabeth-Jane does indeed marry Farfrae.

Chapter 19

Henchard cannot resist telling Elizabeth-Jane what he thinks is the truth – that she is his daughter, not Newson's. While searching for some proof of this, he comes across Susan's letter, which he reads because it has been poorly sealed. He discovers that his child died and that Elizabeth-Jane is Newson's daughter. Henchard resolves not to tell Elizabeth-Jane, and she accepts him as her father.

Elizabeth-Jane both loses and gains a father
The loss of Susan by death, Farfrae by 'estrangement' and Elizabeth-Jane's ignorance that he is her true father, prey on Henchard's mind. He wishes to reclaim his daughter and, driven by loneliness and his need to express love, he tells Elizabeth-Jane that he, not Newson, is her father.

Note how, despite her efforts to 'confront him trustfully', Elizabeth-Jane is still 'troubled at his presence'. Henchard, buffeted by the cruel blows of chance and fate as well as by the results of his own actions, is described as a 'great tree in a wind'. Ironically, his search for proof of Elizabeth-Jane's parentage leads him to open Susan's badly sealed letter, and to discover that Elizabeth-Jane *is* Newson's daughter. Note Henchard's reaction to the discovery – it is as though the letter were a 'window-pane through which he saw for miles'. Suddenly Susan's past conduct becomes clear to him – but too late!

Henchard's loneliness and suffering are apparent in the mood of his walk along the river bank. Look at the words and images used – 'mournful phases', 'torturing cramps', 'pined', 'slow, noiseless, and dark', 'voice of desolation', the corpse of a man'.

Chapter 20

Bitterly disappointed that she is not his daughter, Henchard finds fault in everything that Elizabeth-Jane does, despite her attempts at self-improvement. While tending her mother's grave she meets a young woman who suggests she should come to live with her as her companion. Henchard, anxious to rid himself of Newson's daughter, writes to Farfrae to tell him he no longer has any objection to his seeing Elizabeth-Jane.

Henchard rejects Elizabeth-Jane

Henchard is cold towards Elizabeth-Jane, finding fault in her use of dialect words and lack of formal education. His disappointment is hardly her fault, yet he blames her – his is not a rational mind, but one driven by quick emotions, judgements and decisions. Perhaps his great fault is a tendency to self-pity.

Susan's fears in Chapter 8 that the mayor's pride would be damaged if he ever discovered that Elizabeth-Jane had worked at the Three Mariners are confirmed when Nance Mockridge reveals this to Henchard.

Elizabeth-Jane fails to understand the reasons for Henchard's hostility. Ashamed of her lack of education, she strives hard to remedy it and lives a lonely life, repressing her interest in Farfrae, who never seems to notice her.

The seeds of Henchard's downfall

Henchard's fortunes continue to decline. His period as Mayor of Casterbridge is about to end, and he discovers he will not be invited to become an alderman. His frustration when he learns that Farfrae *will* be invited is increased by the knowledge, recently obtained, that it was Farfrae to whom Elizabeth-Jane had served dinner at The Three Mariners.

> The meeting of Lucetta and Elizabeth-Jane contains strong parallels with earlier incidents. Henchard confided his story to a complete stranger, but unwittingly left out key elements of the story, Elizabeth-Jane does the same here. Both the people in whom they confide turn out to be rivals: Farfrae for Henchard's business; Lucetta for Farfrae's hand. Farfrae immediately moved into Henchard's house and Elizabeth-Jane moves in with Lucetta.

Chapter 21

Elizabeth-Jane goes to look at High-Place Hall and nearly runs into Henchard, who is also showing an interest in the place. She leaves her home in Corn Street to live with Lucetta Templeman. When Henchard realises how Elizabeth-Jane has tried to improve herself, he is greatly moved and asks her to stay, but his request comes ten minutes too late.

Elizabeth-Jane moves out

Setting

Lucetta Templeman

Henchard seems indifferent to Elizabeth-Jane's announcement of her departure. Why, then, doesn't he complete the break by telling her about Newson? Something holds him back. His offer of money does not resolve his moral obligations to her, any more than it did when he tried the same approach with both Susan and Lucetta.

Lucetta's motives in asking Elizabeth-Jane to stay with her are revealed in her agitation when Elizabeth-Jane mentions that she has not told her father where she is moving to. Lucetta wanted her to stay in order to attract Henchard to her house.

Henchard's impulsiveness again gets him into trouble. When he sees the efforts Elizabeth-Jane has made to improve herself, he regrets having spoken so roughly to her and asks her to stay, but once again he is too late. It is obvious from Henchard's reaction that he knows who else lives at High-Place Hall.

Chapter 22

Henchard's visit to High-Place Hall the previous evening is explained. Lucetta writes to him to say that she has moved to Casterbridge. He realises that his confusion about her identity was because she has taken her aunt's name, Templeman. Lucetta writes to Henchard again, but when he visits her she refuses to see him until the next day. He is rather annoyed at this and puts off his visit for several days. Lucetta learns of the coldness between Elizabeth-Jane and Henchard and realises that she will have to get rid of the girl. A visitor is shown in and Lucetta, thinking it is Henchard, hides behind a curtain.

Henchard and Lucetta pursue their own desires

By means of another letter, we are told of Lucetta's plan to marry Henchard, which, fortunately, coincides with his own plans at this time. He needs to fill the emotional void left by the loss of Elizabeth-Jane, and also wishes to marry Lucetta because he feels he owes it to her. There is also a mercenary element, as he believes she may have some wealth.

It is interesting to note that, like Susan, Lucetta has acquired a new surname. Note the calculated way in which Lucetta assesses the advantages of a marriage to Henchard: she wants to re-establish her social position. She

wanted Elizabeth-Jane to stay so that Henchard would have a reason for visiting High-Place Hall. Lucetta's scheme echoes Susan's plan to use Henchard's ignorance of Elizabeth-Jane's real father to get her into Henchard's home. Neither plan works out quite as hoped.

Narrative devices

The view of the marketplace from the window of High-Place Hall is another example of the narrative device of framing a scene. Note the many details which are described and commented on, building a picture of the business activities of Casterbridge.

Setting

Lucetta's timidity

Lucetta discovers Henchard's estrangement from Elizabeth-Jane and realises that

High-Place Hall is the one place he will avoid. Driven by Henchard's non-appearance to write another letter to him, Lucetta arranges herself on a chair in an affected pose while waiting for him to arrive. But she hides behind the curtains when she hears a visitor arriving. Be aware of how easily she is upset, since this prepares us for a more traumatic event later in the story. Suspense is created when Lucetta comes out to discover that her visitor is not Henchard after all.

Self-test (Questions) Chapters 13–22

Uncover the plot
Delete two of the three alternatives given, to find the correct plot. Beware possible misconceptions and muddles.
Henchard courts and marries Lucetta/Susan/Miss Le Sueur; Elizabeth-Jane flourishes in her new life as does Farfrae's/Henchard's/Jopp's business under Jopp/Henchard/Farfrae. Proud/jealous/ignorant of Farfrae's success and popularity, Henchard dismisses/promotes/ignores him. When Farfrae sets up his own business the rivalry intensifies, and Henchard forbids the development of an incipient intimacy between Farfrae and Elizabeth-Jane/Susan and Farfrae/Farfrae and Lucetta. Susan dies and Henchard tells Elizabeth-Jane that he, not Newson, is her father; however, a letter left by/forged by/stolen from Susan informs the Mayor that Newson was the father. Henchard takes against Elizabeth-Jane, who goes to live with Henchard's former fiancée/wife/employee as her companion.

Who? What? Why? When? How?
1 What is the 'circular disc reticulated with creases' that Longways sees?
2 When Susan and Henchard marry, what does Henchard want Elizabeth-Jane to do?
3 How does Farfrae look at Elizabeth-Jane and Susan, and why?
4 Why do Elizabeth-Jane and Farfrae both arrive at the granary?
5 How does Henchard force Abel Whittle to dress at work; why, and what is Farfrae's reaction?
6 Why does Henchard's entertainment fail?
7 Who was it that sent Elizabeth-Jane and Farfrae to the granary, and why?
8 What kind of father does Elizabeth-Jane say Newson was?.
9 According to Susan, when did Henchard's real daughter die?
10 In her letter to Henchard, what reason does Lucetta give for inviting Elizabeth-Jane to live with her?

Who is this?
From your knowledge of the characters in the novel, identify the following people.
1 Who is 'masterful and coercive'?
2 Who is 'reasonable' in almost everything she does?
3 Who is 'as kind to (Susan) as a man, mayor and churchwarden could possibly be'?
4 Who is the most admired man in Casterbridge?
5 Who are described as 'fine old crusted characters'?
6 Who is the 'dirk' and who the 'cudgel' in the commercial rivalry between Henchard and Farfrae, and what does the comparison reveal about their characters?
7 Who is characterised by 'honesty in dishonesty'?
8 Who 'read omnivorously'?
9 Who has a 'flexuous gait' and is 'simply pretty'?
10 Who is younger than her companion, but more of a 'sage'?

Fatal attraction
The role of irony/fate/destiny is developed in this section. With this in mind, answer the following questions.
1 Why does Elizabeth-Jane not dress 'too gay' when her lifestyle changes?
2 Hardy concurs with Novalis' view that 'character is Fate'; what point is he making with regard to Farfrae and Henchard?
3 What is the 'mockery' of Henchard's situation when he reads Susan's letter, and what does he think of it?
4 What is the irony of Elizabeth-Jane's situation, as she herself perceives it?
5 What might have happened at High-Place Hall had Henchard not chided Elizabeth-Jane about her manner/behaviour?

Apt adjectives

pale	bluebeardy	disdainful	fragile	fiery
reasonable	picturesque	fragile	circumspect	meek
self-conscious	unsophisticated	humble	crude	energetic
chastened	brainy	bright	domineering	flexuous
impetuous	tyrannical	patient	genial	jealous
warm	artistic	sincere	undisciplined	pretty
luminous	accomplished	gloomy	energetic	handsome
vehement	dogged	insightful	choleric	moody
emotional	lonely	self-willed	light-hearted	artful
reckless				

From the above list, choose five adjectives you feel best describe:
1 Elizabeth-Jane
2 Farfrae
3 Henchard
4 Susan
5 Lucetta
You may wish to use the same word for more than one character – but be sure to keep the text closely in mind.

Self-test (Answers) Chapters 13–22

Uncover the plot

Henchard courts and marries Susan; Elizabeth-Jane flourishes in her new life, as does Henchard's business under Farfrae. Jealous of Farfrae's success and popularity, Henchard dismisses him. When Farfrae sets up his own business the rivalry intensifies, and Henchard forbids the development of an incipient intimacy between Farfrae and Elizabeth-Jane. Susan dies and Henchard tells Elizabeth-Jane that he, not Newson, was the father; however, a letter left by Susan informs the Mayor that Newson was the father. Henchard takes against Elizabeth-Jane, who goes to live with Henchard's former fiancée as her companion.

Who? What? Why? When? How?

1 Mrs Cuxsom's face (13)
2 Take his name (13)
3 With 'curious interest'; he knows their story (14)
4 They both receive the same note asking them to go there (14)
5 Without his trousers; he is late for work again; to threaten to leave unless Henchard agreed to send Whittle back home to dress (15)
6 Due to bad weather (16)
7 Susan Henchard; she wanted them to marry (18)
8 Very kind (19)
9 Three months after the auction (19)
10 To give Henchard an excuse to visit and court Lucetta (22)

Who is this?

1 Henchard (13)
2 Elizabeth-Jane (14)
3 Henchard (14)
4 Donald Farfrae (15)
5 The councilmen (16)
6 Farfrae; Henchard; subtlety and brains against brute force and strength (17)
7 Susan (19)
8 Elizabeth-Jane (20)
9 Lucetta (20)
10 Elizabeth-Jane (22)

Fatal attraction

1 'It would be tempting Providence' (14)
2 That Farfrae's character set him up for success, whereas Henchard – a 'vehement gloomy being' – was naturally destined to suffer (17)
3 That as soon as he has taught Elizabeth-Jane to accept him as her father he discovers that she is not his kin; that he has deserved it (19)
4 That her father should reveal himself to her, only to become increasingly cold and distant (19)
5 Elizabeth-Jane might not have hidden from her father, and they might then have asked each other questions and discovered much more about the true situation (21)

Apt adjectives

You could choose any of the following. Bear in mind that this is not a definitive list; you may of course find others that you think are suitable. When in doubt, however, try to back up your choice with a reference to the text.

1 reasonable, circumspect, unsophisticated, patient, sincere, handsome, insightful, subtle-souled, thoughtful, lonely, luminous, self-conscious, disciplined, proper
2 circumspect, energetic, brainy, bright, genial, warm, sincere, accomplished, handsome
3 bluebeardy, disdainful, crude, energetic, domineering, impetuous, tyrannical, jealous, undisciplined, gloomy, dogged, choleric, moody, emotional, lonely, self-willed, reckless
4 pale, fragile, meek, self-conscious, unsophisticated, humble, patient, sincere, chastened
5 picturesque, flexuous, impetuous, artistic, pretty, accomplished, emotional, light-hearted, artful, reckless

Chapter 23

The visitor is Farfrae, who has come to see Elizabeth-Jane. Lucetta is immediately attracted to him. Farfrae prevents two lovers being parted by hiring the young man and his father. Farfrae leaves, having forgotten the reason for his visit. Henchard arrives, but Lucetta refuses to see him, and now, ironically, sees Elizabeth-Jane's presence as a means of keeping Henchard away.

Two of a kind?

Farfrae comes to High-Place Hall to see Elizabeth-Jane, having been granted permission by Henchard. Ironically, it is Lucetta whom he meets and the two are immediately attracted to one another. Henchard's delay in visiting Lucetta leads to this new situation. Lucetta's declaration that she is lonely conveniently ignores the presence of Elizabeth-Jane. Notice how Farfrae suddenly decides to tell her the details of his business successes. It could be argued that Farfrae and Lucetta are attracted to one another because they are both shallow, calculating and over-sentimental. Lucetta warns Farfrae against listening to gossip about her. These fears will prove well-founded.

Echoes of the past

Framed by the window, the view of the 'hiring fair' provides us with an interesting situation. The auctioning of someone's services to the highest bidder, which in this case is likely to result in the separation of the young man and his sweetheart, is a reminder of another auction many years ago at Weydon-Priors.

An opportunity missed

Yet again, Henchard arrives on the scene just too late to retrieve a situation which might have altered his future. Is he doomed by fate always to take the wrong path, or does his own character work against him?

Lucetta plans to let Elizabeth-Jane stay in order to keep Henchard away. Does everyone use and manipulate Elizabeth-Jane to suit their own purposes? Was Susan the only character who had her welfare at heart? Certainly Lucetta and Henchard allow their own plans to come before Elizabeth-Jane's welfare, but what of Farfrae? Does he 'use' her for his own gain?

Chapter 24

Lucetta and Elizabeth-Jane live for market days, when they can catch a glimpse of Farfrae. One Saturday a new machine arrives in Casterbridge and the two women go to inspect it. When they encounter Farfrae, Elizabeth-Jane senses an attraction between him and Lucetta. Later, Lucetta tells a story about a woman who was promised to one man but has since met another, whom she prefers. Elizabeth-Jane refuses to pass judgement but guesses that the woman in question is Lucetta.

Reactions to the new horse-drill

Setting

The novel is set in the years immediately preceding the repeal of the Corn Laws and the changing face of agriculture is shown by the arrival of the horse-drill in Casterbridge, where it causes a sensation.

Lucetta appeared to be the 'only appropriate possessor of the new machine' because only she 'rivalled it in colour'. The machine causes a sensation in the town and later so will Lucetta.

Henchard ridicules the new machine, perhaps because he represents the old order which resents change. But remember his admiration for Farfrae's new methods in managing his own corn business: is he inconsistent?

Elizabeth-Jane's reaction to the new horse-drill shows that she accepts the inevitability of change, but regrets the passing of the old ways. The reader senses the author's sympathy with her view.

Chapter 25

Both Farfrae and Henchard call on Lucetta, and although the latter offers to marry her she puts off a decision. Both men show total indifference to Elizabeth-Jane, who suffers her rejection silently.

Elizabeth-Jane narrates

In this chapter we see much of the action through Elizabeth-Jane's eyes. She is possessed by a 'seer's spirit' which enables her to observe the developing relationship between Lucetta and Farfrae.

Elizabeth-Jane now realises the identity of both the men in Lucetta's story. She accepts the loss of Farfrae with resignation and misses her 'father', not understanding why he continues to neglect her. Her assessment of the reasons for Henchard's love for Lucetta 'the artificially stimulated coveting of old age' and Farfrae's 'the unforced passion of youth' shows her analytical mind.

Henchard's 'property'

Note how possessive Henchard is towards Lucetta — 'as almost his property'. It reminds us of how he auctioned his wife and child as if they were his property to be disposed of as he wished.

Is Henchard capable of doing anything right? He visited Lucetta in order to court her, yet he ends up arguing with her!

Chapter 26

Henchard suspects that Farfrae is his rival in love, and hires Joshua Jopp as his manager to cut Farfrae out by fair competition. Jopp is only too pleased to do this as he has a grudge against Farfrae. Henchard goes to consult a weather prophet before he puts his plan into operation and is told that the harvest will be washed out. He buys up as much grain as possible, hoping to sell it later at a profit. The weather looks as though it will be fine and Henchard is forced to sell at a loss, for which he blames Joshua Jopp and dismisses him.

Selfish desires and plans

The short conversation between Henchard and Farfrae is ironic. Henchard, wrapped up in his own thoughts, failed at his last meeting with Lucetta to see where her affections now lie. His questioning of Farfrae shows he is unaware that Farfrae is the cause of Lucetta's refusal to marry him. Farfrae, deep in reading Lucetta's letter, fails to make the connection between the woman whom Henchard is talking about and Lucetta. It seems that all of the characters except Elizabeth-Jane are so bound up in their own selfish desires that they fail to notice events which will frustrate them.

One of the most humorous scenes in the novel is the one in which Lucetta and her two suitors take tea together. Elizabeth-Jane's comment: 'How ridiculous of all three of them!' is an apt comment on their stupidity and selfishness.

Mr Jopp, Henchard's new manager

The mingling of business rivalry with rivalry in love is the major factor in persuading Henchard that he needs to do something drastic about Farfrae. His appointment of Jopp is misguided and, ironically, will lead not to the downfall of Farfrae but to the death of Lucetta — the woman Henchard wants to marry. Note that Jopp was apparently in Jersey at the same time as Henchard. It is Jopp who will make the contents of Lucetta's letters known.

Her assessment of Jopp as the wrong man for the job shows Elizabeth-Jane's shrewdness. She also shows spirit in the way she tackles Henchard on the subject.

Mr Fall – weather prophet

An agricultural town like Casterbridge was entirely dependent on the wheat crop, which in turn depended on the weather. The weather was therefore central to every man's thoughts.

Mr Fall, the weather prophet, makes a comfortable living by predicting the weather, although no one will admit to believing in his forecasts. Henchard's visit to the weather prophet contrasts the business attitudes of Henchard and Farfrae – it is doubtful whether Farfrae would ever even consider seeking such advice. At a time of crisis at the start of the story, Henchard went to church and vowed to change, but he had control over that vow. At this new time of crisis he goes to a very dubious source for advice, and he will have no control over the outcome.

'Act in haste'

The dismissal of Jopp is a serious error of judgement on Henchard's part. Jopp had no reason to like Farfrae, having lost his job as manager to him, and now Farfrae's success means Jopp has lost his job again. However, he has just as many reasons for hating Henchard – remember his brusque dismissal by Henchard when he first applied for the job as corn-manager, and this second dismissal leaves him nursing a grievance against both Henchard and Farfrae.

Chapter 27

No sooner does the harvest begin than the rains come, proving the weather prophet right after all. Rivalry between Henchard and Farfrae grows and is taken up by their men. Henchard follows Lucetta, and Farfrae overhears their conversation. Henchard visits Lucetta later in the evening and, by threatening to reveal their past relationship, forces her to promise to marry him. Elizabeth-Jane is called as a witness.

Henchard's plans come to nothing

Despite the disaster that he has suffered and the success of his rival Farfrae, Henchard is unable to believe that Farfrae had any hand in his misfortune. There is an almost perverse contrariness in Henchard's attitude to Farfrae, Lucetta and Elizabeth-Jane. Here, when you might most expect him to rail against Farfrae, he descends instead into a 'moody depression'. Perhaps he feels that it is not man but fate which contends against him.

> The fight between the two waggoners foreshadows the fight between Henchard and Farfrae. The overturning of Henchard's hay in front of Elizabeth-Jane and Lucetta is also symbolic. The whole of Henchard's world will soon tumble down, just like his hay.

A marriage 'contract'

Henchard, feeling that he is about to lose the last 'thing' available to him, forces Lucetta to promise to marry him, by threatening to reveal her past. It is ironic that Lucetta, a keen letter-writer, is being blackmailed by her own letters – or so it seems.

Henchard needs Elizabeth-Jane to witness Lucetta's response, presumably to ensure the fulfilment of the verbal contract, but she also witnesses his harshness and Lucetta's reluctance, preparing the way for her final rejection of him.

Secrets

The accusation from Elizabeth-Jane against Lucetta: 'You have many secrets from me' touches on one of the key reasons why so many of the characters' plans fail to succeed. Every character in the novel is affected by the secrets and deceits of their own or of others' making.

Chapter 28

By coincidence, Henchard is presiding at the magistrate's court where the furmity woman from Weydon-Priors fair is being tried. She reveals how Henchard sold his wife and daughter. Lucetta hears of the story and is worried about the promise of the previous evening. She goes away for a few days' rest.

The furmity woman reveals all

Henchard's 'rough and ready perceptions', so well suited to the simple cases he deals with in court, are not up to the complications of his own life. Has he dealt justly with Farfrae, Susan, Lucetta, Elizabeth-Jane, Jopp, or Whittle?

Fate intervenes with the reappearance of the old furmity woman and the circumstances which lead Henchard to stand in for Dr Chalkfield as a magistrate. This will not be the furmity woman's last appearance in the novel, but for

Henchard it is the catastrophe towards which events and fate seem to have been moving. The one secret, which up till now he has been able to conceal, is made public in the most spectacular way. Almost fatalistically, he makes no attempt to deny the furmity woman's allegations, merely acknowledging their truth. This is the crux of the novel for Henchard. With the exposure of his major secret, his fall is guaranteed.

Chapter 29

Lucetta is walking along the Port Bredy road when she meets Elizabeth-Jane. The two women are chased into a barn by a bull and it is Henchard who saves them and subdues the animal. Henchard takes the hysterical Lucetta home and learns that she has already married Farfrae in Port Bredy.

Henchard rescues Lucetta, but she cannot rescue him

The violence with which Henchard controls the bull suggests the lack of finesse with which he approaches personal relationships. It is ironic that in rescuing the two women from the bull, Henchard takes great care over the hysterical Lucetta, who is already the wife of his rival, while ignoring Elizabeth-Jane, who will be his only comfort in the future.

Henchard attempts to use his relationship with Lucetta to demonstrate his creditworthiness. This reflects the incident with Susan at the start of the novel. He used Susan to acquire money and 'lost' her as a result. His attempt to use Lucetta to gain credit will be followed very swiftly by the realisation that he has lost her as well.

Chapter 30

Lucetta discloses her marriage to Elizabeth-Jane and asks her to stay on at High-Place Hall. Elizabeth-Jane is shocked at her impropriety and immediately takes lodgings on her own.

Elizabeth-Jane – alone

Farfrae sends Lucetta ahead homewards from Port Bredy because he has business to attend to and because he feels that Lucetta is in the best position to break the news to the 'inmates' of her house. From pleasure at the thought of Lucetta's marriage to her father, to distress at her actual marriage to Farfrae, Elizabeth-Jane's world is in a turmoil. Could she reasonably have stayed in the same house as Lucetta and Farfrae, given her pursuit of respectability? Now she has to fall back on

her own resources. Note the casual way that Lucetta accepts her departure. She shows little concern for Elizabeth-Jane's welfare, only about her own problems and worries. She has married Farfrae without telling him the secrets of her past.

Chapter 31

Henchard is declared a bankrupt, and at the hearing he acts fairly and even sells his gold watch to pay the poorest of his creditors. He goes to live in Jopp's cottage, giving orders that he wishes to see no one. Even Elizabeth-Jane is turned away. Farfrae takes over Henchard's business, where he continues to be popular, despite working the men harder and paying them less.

Henchard's final fall

Events beyond Henchard's control play a part in his downfall, when one of his men misrepresents the quality of some corn, compromising Henchard badly. There will shortly be another 'fillip downward' when the period of his vow of abstinence runs out.

The story began with an auction by means of which Henchard acquired the determination to succeed in life. Now he auctions everything he has and seems to have nothing left, morally, spiritually or physically. The gloomy atmosphere of Jopp's cottage near the Priory Mill is a fitting backdrop to his despair.

A new master and new ways of work

Abel Whittle contrasts life in the corn stores before and after Farfrae's takeover: Farfrae pays less and expects hard work, but the men are not afraid of him and go to work with lighter hearts. The triumph of the new scientific farming methods over the old ways is evident from the use of scales and steelyards for measuring where guesswork had formerly been the rule. The change reflects the differences between Henchard and Farfrae, and the changes taking place in the community.

Chapter 32

Henchard spends much of his time standing brooding on the two bridges with other unfortunates. Jopp tells him that Farfrae has moved into his old house and bought up his furniture. Henchard refuses Farfrae's assistance. He falls ill and is comforted by

Elizabeth-Jane, who gives him some hope for the future. Farfrae gives him employment in his old trade but, hearing that Farfrae is to be proposed as mayor, Henchard's resentment increases and he begins to look forward to the end of his vow of abstinence.

Jopp's pleasure and Farfrae's 'business arrangements'

Jopp takes pleasure in telling Henchard about Farfrae's purchase of his house and furniture – Jopp's presence always seems to threaten trouble. Farfrae offers Henchard accommodation and shows him great kindness. Does it appear that Farfrae has discussed this matter with Lucetta? It may be a kindness to Henchard, but what would it have been to Lucetta? Contrast the generosity Farfrae shows towards Henchard, and the lack of it in his business dealings and in his relationships with Lucetta and Elizabeth-Jane. Perhaps he sees the two women as part of his 'business' arrangements?

Echoes of the past

Compare this meeting between the two men with their first meeting – Henchard is offered lodgings, a job and even a meal. Henchard is unable to come to terms with his loss of status and continues to wear his suit rather than the traditional dress of the hay-trusser. The release of Henchard from his vow of abstinence sets the seal on his downfall. There remains but one thing for him to lose: the respect and love of Elizabeth-Jane.

Chapter 33

Henchard, now free from his oath, drinks in the Three Mariners. One Sunday, he bullies the choir into singing a psalm with threatening words, directed at Farfrae. Elizabeth-Jane takes him home, but his threats make her feel that it is her duty to warn Farfrae. Henchard is unkind to Lucetta, who incriminates herself with another letter asking him to refrain from speaking to her in such a way.

The scene at the Three Mariners Inn is reminiscent of the occasion when Farfrae sang there. But now there is little goodwill and mutual respect to be found. Henchard's violent temper is evident when he forces the choir to sing a psalm which seems to attack Farfrae.

> Henchard's observation that when he was rich he did not need what he could have, but now he is poor he cannot have what he needs is similar to that of Elizabeth-Jane in Chapter 25: 'what she had desired had not been granted her, and that what had been granted her she had not desired'. But Henchard refers to material things whilst the phrase describing Elizabeth-Jane relates to relationships and emotions.

■ Self-test (Questions) Chapters 23–33

Uncover the plot

Delete two of the three alternatives given, to find the correct plot. Beware possible misconceptions and muddles.

Lucetta and Jopp/Henchard/Farfrae fall in love. Henchard continues to court Lucetta; learning the identity of his new rival he re-employs the friendly/prosperous/slighted Jopp to help him cut out Farfrae from the corn trade. The two of them bet on a good/indifferent/bad harvest in error and Jopp is promoted/praised/dismissed. Henchard threatens to reveal the truth about their past relationship unless Lucetta agrees to marry him; she refuses/agrees/is thrilled, but when the old furmity woman makes public the story of the auction, Lucetta runs away/marries Farfrae in secret/falls ill. Elizabeth-Jane leaves the house. Henchard's goods are repossessed and he moves in with Jopp/Farfrae/the Mayor. Farfrae, tipped for Mayor, employs Henchard in his yard. Henchard – his 10-/21-/2-year-old vow to abstain from women/alcohol/politics at an end – turns once more to drink.

Who? What? Why? When? How?

1 Why are Lucetta and Elizabeth-Jane always to be found at home on Saturdays?
2 Who is the 'odd one out' when Farfrae comes to High-Place Hall?
3 What is Henchard's reason for sending for Jopp, and what condition is Jopp in?
4 Who is 'Mr Fall', and what does Henchard's visit to him reveal about the Mayor's character?
5 When does the weather deteriorate, and what would have happened had Henchard been more patient?
6 Who is put on trial at the Town Hall, and why?
7 What chases Elizabeth-Jane and Lucetta, and who saves them?
8 How does Henchard find out about the secret wedding?
9 What does Elizabeth-Jane say Lucetta should do, in all propriety?
10 Why does Henchard go to live with Jopp?

Who is this?

From your knowledge of the characters in the novel, identify the following people.
1 'I am a very ambitious woman.'
2 'She had learned the lesson of renunciation.'
3 'He was well-nigh ferocious at the sense of the queer situation in which he stood towards this woman.'
4 'He has such a knack of making everything bring him fortune.'
5 The man whose clothing spoke of 'neediness' and who would not 'stick at trifles'.
6 The 'old flagrant female, swearing and committing a nuisance'.
7 'Her craving for correctness of procedure was, indeed, almost vicious.'
8 '... how admirably he had used his one talent of energy to create a position of affluence out of absolutely nothing.'
9 'A feeling of delicacy... prompted (him) to avoid anything that might seem like triumphing over a fallen rival'.
10 'Poor fool! To know no better than commit herself in writing like this!'

Prove it!

Find a quote in the text that backs up the following statements.
1 When declared bankrupt, Henchard conducts himself honourably. (31)
2 The romance of agriculture is lost as a result of technical innovation and development. (24)
3 The town would have been less judgmental of Henchard if his past had been known from the start. (31)
4 Elizabeth-Jane was Henchard's only true friend. (31)
5 Henchard is aware that he has acted wrongly with regard to Farfrae. (32)

Uncover the plot

Lucetta and Farfrae fall in love. Henchard continues to court Lucetta; learning he identity of his new rival he re-employs the slighted Jopp to help him cut out Farfrae from the corn trade. The two of them bet on a bad harvest in error and Jopp is dismissed. Henchard threatens to reveal the truth about the past unless Lucetta agrees to marry him; she agrees, but when the old furmity woman makes public the story of the auction, Lucetta marries Farfrae in secret. Elizabeth-Jane leaves the house. Henchard's goods are repossessed and he moves in with Jopp. Farfrae, tipped for Mayor, employs Henchard in his yard. Henchard – his 21-year-old vow to abstain from alcohol at an end – turns once more to drink.

Who? What? Why? When? How?

1 Saturday is market-day, and they both watch out for Farfrae (24)
2 Elizabeth-Jane (25)
3 He plans to employ Jopp to help him bid against Farfrae; poor and needy (26)
4 A weather forecaster; that Henchard is superstitious (26)
5 As soon as Henchard has sold his corn; he could have avoided such a serious loss (27)
6 The old furmity woman from the Fair; for drunk and disorderly conduct (28)
7 A bull; Henchard (29)
8 He asks Lucetta to help him stall a creditor; Lucetta has to refuse because the creditor was a witness at her marriage (29)
9 Marry Mr Henchard, or no man (30)
10 Because his goods have been repossessed, and Jopp is the only man whose opinion he despises to the point of indifference (32)

Who is this?

1 Lucetta (23)
2 Elizabeth-Jane (25)
3 Henchard (26)
4 Farfrae (26)
5 Jopp (26)
6 The furmity seller (27)
7 Elizabeth-Jane (30)
8 Henchard (31)
9 Farfrae (33)
10 Lucetta (33)

Prove it!

1 'I have never met a debtor who behaved more fairly' (31)
2 'Then the romance of the sower is gone for good' (24)
3 'Had the incident been well known of old and always, it might by this time have grown to be lightly regarded' (31)
4 'She believed in him still, though nobody else did' (31)
5 'I – sometimes think I've wronged 'ee!' (32)

Chapter 34

Elizabeth-Jane warns Farfrae of Henchard's hatred towards him, but he dismisses her fears. However, when the information is confirmed by someone else, he abandons a plan to set Henchard up in a seedman's shop. Lucetta asks Henchard to return her old letters and he remembers that they are in his safe in the house now occupied by Farfrae and Lucetta. He goes there that evening, intending to disclose the contents to Farfrae but, although he reads some of the letters out loud, he hasn't the heart to reveal the name of the sender.

A threat to Farfrae

Although at first Farfrae dismisses Elizabeth-Jane's fears that Henchard means him harm, he later begins to take the threat seriously. Note his lack of feeling and respect in speaking to her with 'the cheeriness of a superior'.

In the midst of carrying out an act of kindness, Farfrae learns of Henchard's bitterness. Consider carefully Farfrae's comment 'what harm have I done him that he should try to wrong me?' Has he knowingly done Henchard any harm? Could he have acted with more sensitivity, or is there nothing in his life but success in business?

Farfrae's advancement

Lucetta's plan to leave Casterbridge is upset by the news that Farfrae has been offered the position of mayor. He often invokes Providence, but what do you think is his real attitude towards fate? Now Farfrae has completely replaced Henchard – as successful corn-factor and as Mayor of Casterbridge. As he has risen, so Henchard has fallen. Is this a matter of coincidence alone?

Some letters to read

Note the use of grim, ironic humour to make the reading of Lucetta's letters to Farfrae more dramatic. Even in his depressed and angry mood, Henchard cannot quite bring himself to destroy Lucetta. It is perhaps strange that Farfrae does not put two and two together here. At the very least he should wonder why Henchard flaunts the letters. Perhaps his self-centred feelings make him immune to doubt and blunt his curiosity.

Chapter 35

Lucetta has overheard Henchard reading out some of the letters. She writes to him again and pleads with him to return them. They arrange to meet at the Ring and the surroundings remind him of his treatment of Susan. He promises to return the letters.

Lucetta threatened

Farfrae's advice to Henchard to burn the letters is ignored – with disastrous results for everyone. Again, Lucetta's tendency to become hysterical when under pressure prepares us for later events.

Lucetta finds it impossible to tell Farfrae the truth. She wants to escape rather than accept responsibility for her past, because she believes that he would see her relationship with Henchard as 'her fault rather than her misfortune'.

> Events come full circle with the return of Henchard to the Ring to meet the other woman in his life. Just as Susan wanted something from Henchard, so now does Lucetta. Henchard is jealous of Lucetta's love for Farfrae, even though he can now see her vulnerability. Henchard's attempts to achieve a loving relationship seem to be frustrated just as he is about to grasp the opportunity.

Chapter 36

As Lucetta returns home from her meeting with Henchard, she meets Jopp who asks her to recommend him as manager to Farfrae. She dismisses him. Henchard asks Jopp to deliver the package of letters to Lucetta, but on his way there Jopp calls at the Peter's Finger. The package is opened and the contents disclosed to the assembled company. They arrange a skimmington ride to punish Lucetta for her impropriety. The letters are repackaged and delivered to Lucetta, who immediately burns them. Meanwhile, a stranger arrives in Casterbridge.

Jopp and Jersey

The presence of Jopp threatens trouble once again. Lucetta's refusal to speak favourably of him to Farfrae makes him eager for revenge. The references that Jopp makes to Jersey, to both Henchard and Lucetta, pose a threat to them, and create suspense in the narrative.

Henchard wants to free Lucetta from her past indiscretions, so he agrees to return her letters and asks Jopp to deliver them. In parcelling up the letters he fails to seal them properly – the author used the device of badly sealed letters earlier, when Henchard learned the true parentage of Elizabeth-Jane.

Jopp and the furmity woman

Setting

The description of Mixen Lane as the home of those in distress and debt completes our view of Casterbridge society. The changing face of rural Wessex is illustrated by reference to the families of decayed villages, now deprived them of homes which had been theirs for generations. The furmity woman makes her last appearance and again sets events in motion by asking Jopp what is in the parcel he carries.

A stranger arrives
Another stranger arrives in Casterbridge. His shout of 'ahoy' and the ease with which he 'walked the plank' should remind us of the sailor at the start of the story.

Chapter 37
Henchard asks the council if he can join them in welcoming a visiting royal personage, but is refused. On the day, Henchard appears in his shabby clothes, waving a flag, and is roughly ordered away by Farfrae. Lucetta is goaded by the talk of some of the other women. The skimmington ride has been planned for that night.

Two interesting 'rides'
There is an irony in the contrast between the two sets of preparations that are going on here: one for the skimmington ride, and the other for the ride of a royal personage through the town. Both events represent different stages in the development of Casterbridge, and in the fortunes of Lucetta and Henchard. One reflects the town's history, the other its future. One will lead to Lucetta's death the other to the degradation and death of Henchard.

Coming to terms with change

There is something pathetic yet defiant in the appearance of Henchard, dressed in 'weather-beaten garments of bygone years', contrasting with the rest of the Casterbridge folk. It emphasises the fate of those who are unable to come to terms with change. The triumph of Farfrae and Lucetta is not popular with the townsfolk. Christopher Coney remarks that Farfrae has lost some of the charm he had when he came to Casterbridge as a 'light-hearted, penniless youth'.

Chapter 38
Henchard wants revenge on Farfrae and asks for a meeting in the granary. He binds one of his arms because he is the stronger man and, when Farfrae arrives, starts to fight him. Henchard overpowers Farfrae but cannot bring himself to kill him, and is later ashamed of himself. Farfrae goes to Weatherbury, summoned by an anonymous letter.

Henchard's last desperate blow against his fate

Although Henchard hates Farfrae and has decided to kill him, he wants to make the fight fair, so he binds one of his arms to his side. The catalogue of 'insults' which Henchard recites does not justify an attempt to kill Farfrae and at heart Henchard knows this, just as he knew that he could not tell Farfrae the name of the person who wrote the letters Henchard read to him. There are boundaries of decency beyond which he will not go.

Chapter 39

An anonymous letter has been sent by Longways and some of Farfrae's other men, in an attempt to lure him away from the scene of the skimmington ride. Lucetta hears the approach of the procession and, although Elizabeth-Jane appears and tries to prevent her from seeing it, she fails – Lucetta becomes hysterical and insists on looking out. When she sees the effigies, she has a fit. The procession disappears.

The skimmington ride

Farfrae's popularity with his men is evident from their attempt to get him out of the way by sending him an anonymous letter.

The skimmington ride's effect on Lucetta is sharpened by its contrast with her illusion of security now that she has destroyed her incriminating letters. The description of the clothing worn by the effigies leaves Lucetta in no doubt about whom they are intended to represent and, although Elizabeth-Jane tries to protect her friend from the spectacle, Lucetta's attempts to hide the truth and escape her past only lead her to incriminate herself further.

Chapter 40

On seeing the skimmington ride, Henchard follows Elizabeth-Jane to Farfrae's house. He learns of Lucetta's illness and of the doctor's request for Farfrae to come immediately. Realising that Farfrae has changed his plans, Henchard goes to find him, but Farfrae refuses to trust him. When he does return home, Farfrae is distressed both by his mistrust of Henchard and by his wife's condition. Lucetta dies after revealing her secret. Henchard returns home to discover that a sea-captain had called to see him.

Henchard is rejected

Henchard is filled with remorse at the thought of his attack upon Farfrae. But when he tries to make amends, no one trusts him. The irony of this is stressed by a biblical allusion to Job who, when brought to justice for his crimes, cursed 'the day in which he was born, the night during which he was conceived, and his whole existence'.

In his despair, Henchard sees hope in Elizabeth-Jane and resolves to love her, even though she is not his daughter.

The stranger returns

Our suspicions that the stranger to Casterbridge might be Newson are strengthened when Jopp tells Henchard that a sea-captain of some sort had called. Note the cruelty of fate. Just when Henchard has resolved to love Elizabeth-Jane, a threat from the past emerges.

Deception

Chapter 41

Elizabeth-Jane visits Henchard to inform him of Lucetta's death. He sees that she is tired and encourages her to rest while he makes some breakfast. Newson the sea-captain calls to enquire about Elizabeth-Jane and Henchard tells him she is dead. Newson accepts his word and leaves Casterbridge. Henchard immediately regrets his lie but, filled with fear of losing Elizabeth-Jane's love, he resolves to keep the truth from her. Elizabeth-Jane offers to come and live with him.

Elizabeth-Jane's father returns

Elizabeth-Jane ponders on the appalling unexpectedness of Lucetta's death amid such promise of happiness. It is ironic that she should think this, comfortably settled as she is on a couch in her 'father's' lodgings, given the events which are about to unfold. Similarly, Henchard dreams of a future 'lit by her filial presence', even though he knows her 'filial presence' is a lie of his own and Susan's making.

The stranger in Casterbridge reveals himself as Newson. His reappearance may seem contrived, but he is the only one who can tell Elizabeth-Jane of her true parentage, something Henchard will never do for fear of losing her love.

Henchard deceives again

These 'mad lies like a child, in pure mockery of consequences' will be the final undoing of Henchard. Amazed himself at the lie he has told Newson, it is typical of him to regret it immediately. His fear of losing Elizabeth-Jane prevents him from accepting responsibility for his actions. Again, Henchard's mood is reflected in the sombreness of the natural setting.

Elizabeth-Jane's 'natural insight' enables her to sense Henchard's desperation, so she offers to live with him, but it does not enable her to divine his secret.

Henchard considers suicide but refrains when he sees the effigy of himself floating in Ten Hatches. Ironically, he is unable to see that his turn will soon come.

Chapter 42

Newson does not return and Henchard settles down with Elizabeth-Jane to run a small seedman's shop bought for him by the council. Farfrae realises that the revelation of Lucetta's secret would have damaged their relationship and now turns his attention to Elizabeth-Jane. Henchard is jealous and fears losing her, but vows not to interfere in their courtship.

Contradictions in character

Farfrae, despite all the tribulations which Henchard has caused, generously assists him to purchase a small business. But another side of Farfrae is shown when his grief for Lucetta is tempered by his discovery of the secrets of her past, which would have interfered with his ambitions.

The idyllic relationship between Elizabeth-Jane and Henchard contains the seeds of disaster. Henchard notices that Elizabeth-Jane is sometimes polite rather than affectionate to him, and his suspicions of the growing relationship between Elizabeth-Jane and Farfrae make him afraid of losing her. He cannot accept that her marriage to Farfrae would be good for her and for himself. However, Henchard vows that he will not interfere in the relationship. Whatever the faults of the man, there are certain rules of conduct which he refuses to disobey – he could not disclose the author of the letters he read to Farfrae, and nor could he bring himself to harm Farfrae physically.

Chapter 43

Henchard sees Newson return and, taking up the clothes and trade of a hay-trusser, leaves Casterbridge in much the same way as he had arrived, a quarter of a century before. Elizabeth-Jane receives a note from a stranger who wants to meet her at Farfrae's house. Arriving there, she is reunited with her father. She learns how Henchard has prevented her father from seeing her until now, and she turns against Henchard.

Reunited

The locals of the Three Mariners voice their approval of the match between Farfrae and Elizabeth-Jane. Even the once-cynical Christopher Coney admires Elizabeth-Jane. In the passions and conflicts which centre on Henchard, it is easy to overlook Elizabeth-Jane's sufferings. Yet her most testing time is still to come.

The description of prehistoric remains gives a sense of history to the Budmouth road where Farfrae and Elizabeth-Jane meet. It is here, whilst spying on the progress of the romance, that Henchard sees Newson again.

Elizabeth-Jane receives a message that someone wishes to meet her at Farfrae's house. She asks Henchard's permission, which he gives, accepting fatalistically that his secret will soon be known. What do you think would have been the outcome if, at this stage and having nothing to lose, he were to tell Elizabeth-Jane the truth that he has for so long concealed?

Dispossessed

Henchard exchanges his shabby-genteel suit for the clothes of his trade. Compare the way he leaves Casterbridge with his arrival twenty-five years earlier. Does he leave a wiser man?

Newson treats Henchard's lie as a joke, but this is not Elizabeth-Jane's interpretation. Henchard was correct in thinking that there would be no place for him in Casterbridge when the news was broken to his 'daughter'.

Chapter 44

Henchard returns to Weydon-Priors. He obtains work as a hay-trusser and realises he could start again, but he does not have the heart to do so. He learns of the approach of Elizabeth-Jane's wedding day and decides to make one last attempt to seek her forgiveness and love. He returns to Casterbridge and arrives at the wedding festivities. Elizabeth-Jane rejects him and he takes his leave before she can collect her thoughts.

A rejected and lonely man

Henchard sleeps in the open, feeling no hunger. The autumn sun reminds us of events which seem so very long ago now. The few pathetic reminders he has kept of a girl who was unrelated to him are touching indications of how much he loved her.

Henchard returns to the site of the Weydon fair, which reminds him of his past crimes. He recognises his failures and the way ambition destroyed his life. He finds himself in the same position as he was a quarter of a century before, but feels much wiser. Ironically, he no longer has the zest for life that would enable him to profit from his newly acquired wisdom.

Return to Casterbridge

Henchard decides to return to Casterbridge, remembering Elizabeth-Jane's concern that he might miss the wedding and intending to try for her forgiveness. His loneliness is symbolised by his solitary figure on the broad, white highway.

Another wedding – the final one

The voice of Farfrae can be heard rising from the wedding festivities. The author observes, sarcastically, that Farfrae loved his country so much that he never revisited it. It is worth considering whether or not you agree that his love for music and song is only a surface emotion.

Again, a scene is framed by a doorway, emphasising Henchard's exclusion.

Chapter 45

After the wedding, the caged goldfinch which Henchard had brought as a present is found dead from starvation. After several weeks, Elizabeth-Jane discovers that it was Henchard who brought it and she resolves to find him. They search everywhere and are about to give up when they meet Abel Whittle, who tells how he followed Henchard from Casterbridge and looked after him until his death. Henchard left a will pinned to his bed, directing that his memory be forgotten.

Henchard's death

The starved, caged goldfinch perhaps symbolises Henchard, rejected and starved of love. The discovery softens Elizabeth-Jane's heart so that, ironically, Henchard gains too late what he had so earnestly desired.

The tragedy of Henchard's death is emphasised by the pathos of Abel Whittle's loyalty in repaying Henchard for the kindness he showed to Abel's mother. Henchard's final letter makes no attempt to deceive, and asks for no recognition or reward.

Farfrae's priorities

Farfrae's shallowness is indicated by his eagerness to call a halt to the search for Henchard before they are forced to stay overnight somewhere: 'and that will make a hole in a sovereign'. Perhaps more concern for his wife's distress and less for his money might have been appropriate.

Elizabeth-Jane recognises the force of Henchard's last wishes and she carries them out for Henchard's sake, not so that Farfrae can display his 'large-heartedness'. She obviously knows Farfrae's character well and her remark reveals the motives behind all those other occasions when he showed 'large-heartedness'.

Elizabeth-Jane has, by her moderation and practicality, equipped herself to live a happier life. She has learnt through painful experience to accept the indifference of Fate and to make the best of limited opportunities. Although her marriage to Farfrae has brought her much to be thankful for, she is aware of the inevitability of change and the uncertainty of the future.

■ Self-test (Questions) Chapters 34–45

Uncover the plot
Delete two of the three alternatives given, to find the correct plot. Beware possible misconceptions and muddles.

Henchard, despite his hatred/love/fear of Farfrae, does not have the heart to disclose the contents of Lucetta's letters; he sends them back via Clark/Elizabeth-Jane/Jopp, who reveals Lucetta's secret to the townsfolk/her husband/his employer. They arrange a skimmington ride/royal visit/party. Roughly/tactfully/quietly dismissed from Casterbridge's celebrations of the royal visit, Henchard fights and kills/spares/wounds Farfrae, who is then summoned away by an acquaintance/by an anonymous letter/on business. Lucetta falls ill and dies after revealing her secret to Farfrae/Elizabeth-Jane/Newson. Newson, arrived to seek out his daughter/step-daughter/wife, is told of her death by Henchard. Farfrae courts Elizabeth-Jane and Henchard approves/forbids it/leaves Casterbridge. Elizabeth-Jane is reunited with her father and forgives/rejects/welcomes Henchard when he returns. Henchard dies lonely and bitter.

Who? What? Why? When? Where? How?
1 Where does Lucetta meet Henchard to plead with him, and why does this 'unman' him?
2 Where does Jopp say he was for several years, and how many of the novel's characters have been there?
3 How does Jopp manage to read the letters, and what other occasion does this recall?
4 Who finances the skimmington ride, and for what reason?
5 Why does Henchard bind one of his arms?
6 Who sent the anonymous letter to Farfrae, and why?
7 How much of her past does Lucetta tell Farfrae before she dies?
8 What is Henchard's reaction to his own lie to Newson, and what was his main reason for telling it?
9 How does Newson treat Henchard's lie to him, after he is reunited with Elizabeth-Jane; and how does his reaction differ from hers?
10 Why does Abel Whittle care for Henchard?

Who is this?
From your knowledge of the characters in the novel, identify the following people.
1 'Having travelled a great deal in her time she spoke with cosmopolitan largeness of idea.'
2 'For though hers had been rather the laxity of inadvertence than of intention'.
3 '... with practised tact, (he) affected not to have noticed anything unusual.'
4 '... he remained on the sacks in a crouching attitude, unusual for a man, and for such a man.'
5 'Her neck is uncovered, and her hair in bands, and her back-comb in place'.
6 '... in the midst of his gloom she seemed to him as a pin-point of light.'
7 Who spoke 'mad lies like a child, in pure mockery of consequences'?
8 '... the grizzled traveller who had taken Henchard's words on trust so absolute as to shame him as he stood.'
9 Who 'out-Farfraed Farfrae in saltatory intenseness'?
10 Who 'waived his privilege of self-defence'?

Multiple deceptions
Hardy bases the plot of his novel on a series of multiple deceptions. Name FOUR that either occur in this section, or are continued, or resolved.

Significant images
Comment on the significance of the following symbols/images in the novel.
1 The two birds: the swallow in the tent at Weydon-Priors (1); the caged goldfinch (44, 45)
2 The agricultural machine called a horse-drill (24)
3 The two bridges (32)
4 The Ring (11, 35)
5 The bull (29)

Do you agree?
Discuss the following statements briefly.
1 The novel has a happy ending.
2 Farfrae is an admirable man.
3 Henchard deserved to die lonely and bitter.
4 Hardy's characters have the freedom of choice.
5 The author's 'voice' in the novel is highly judgmental of the actions and motives of his characters.

Self-test (Answers) Chapters 34–45

Uncover the plot

Henchard, despite his hatred of Farfrae, does not have the heart to disclose the contents of Lucetta's letters; he sends them back via Jopp, who reveals Lucetta's secret to the townsfolk. They arrange a skimmington ride. Roughly dismissed from Casterbridge's celebrations of the royal visit, Henchard fights and spares Farfrae, who is then summoned away by an anonymous letter. Lucetta falls ill and dies after revealing her secret to Farfrae. Newson, arrived to seek out his daughter, is told of her death by Henchard. Farfrae courts Elizabeth-Jane and Henchard leaves Casterbridge. Elizabeth-Jane is reunited with her father and rejects Henchard when he returns. Henchard dies lonely and bitter.

Who? What? Why? When? Where? How?

1 At the Ring; it reminds him of his meeting there with Susan – another 'ill-used' woman (35)
2 To Jersey; three (Lucetta, Henchard, Jopp) (36)
3 Henchard did not fix the seals properly; Susan failed to seal her letter to Henchard properly, and so he read it and discovered that Elizabeth-Jane was Newson's daughter (36, 19)
4 The stranger (Newson); he wants to see the 'old custom' (36)
5 He is stronger than Farfrae, and wants it to be a fair fight (38)
6 Longways and other of Farfrae's men; to get him out of the way of the skimmington ride (39)
7 It 'cannot be told' – she revealed the bare facts of her relationship with Henchard, but the rest remains Farfrae's secret (40)
8 Amazement; fear of losing Elizabeth-Jane (41)
9 As a joke, well carried out and with no malice behind it; she is angry at the deceit, and resolves not to know Henchard (43)
10 Henchard was kind to his mother (45)

Who is this?

1 The furmity woman (36)
2 Lucetta (36)
3 The royal visitor (37)
4 Henchard (38)
5 The effigy of Lucetta (39)
6 Elizabeth-Jane (40)
7 Henchard (41)
8 Newson (41)
9 Newson (44)
10 Henchard (44)

Multiple deceptions

1 Lucetta continues her deception of Donald, despite Henchard's intentions, only revealing the truth on her death-bed. Even then, the full extent of her disclosure is not known
2 Longways and other of Farfrae's men deceive Farfrae with an anonymous letter, to keep him away from the skimmington ride

3 Henchard deceives Newson, telling him that his daughter died the year before – as well as Elizabeth-Jane, by not informing her of Newson's return
4 Henchard's deception of Elizabeth-Jane as to the identity of her real father is resolved when Newson returns – another anonymous note is involved. Also disclosed is the latter deception of Newson (as to his daughter's death)

Significant images

1 The swallow flies into the tent, and is trapped for a short time. Its efforts to escape distract attention from the auction; had Henchard let the matter drop, the chain of events leading to his death might not have been set in motion. The swallow is in essence free: it 'traps itself' and frees itself. In contrast, there is no escape for the caged finch. Perhaps it is suggested that Henchard descends in the novel from swallow (free to choose) to finch (doomed and to be pitied)?
2 There are mixed reactions to the horse-drill: it represents change, innovation and development – to be both feared and welcomed. It symbolises the threat (hinted at throughout the book) to Wessex' rural communities.
3 Whilst the two bridges are socially divisive, they link all men through their representation of poverty, ill-fortune and death
4 The power of the past (as symbolised by the imposing nature of the place) – as well as change and development – is an important theme. Henchard's past is always haunting him; Lucetta is trapped by hers
5 To some extent Henchard tames himself, as he tames the bull: the bull is violent and threatening, but also trapped and to be pitied

Do you agree?

In your discussion, consider these points (which are suggestions, not definitive answers)
1 The end of the novel is circumspect and cautious: Elizabeth-Jane is not joyfully 'happy', but calm and serene. We have had cause both to doubt Farfrae's qualities and Henchard's deserving of his plight
2 Farfrae is principled, charming and genial; he is also shallow (and perhaps unfeeling?). Unlike Henchard, he is not a man on a 'grand scale'.
3 We are invited to feel ambiguously towards Henchard. He is a complex character: he is at once violent, selfish, energetic and capable of deep love and attachment – in short, we continually reappraise our moral evaluation of him. However you finally judge him, make sure you consider all his qualities
4 While irony of circumstance contributes to the novel's outcome (for example, 'Thus out of error enmity grew' (34) character seems to be each person's destiny. Henchard could have chosen not to sell his wife – but drink, and his wilful obstinacy, would not allow him to back down
5 While Hardy may offer 'opinions' (i.e. 'poor girl'; 'that choleric man'), he does not steer us into making rapid moral judgements. His technique is continually to invite us to appraise and reappraise character, motive and situation

◼ Pairings

Throughout this novel the sensitive reader will be struck by the number of incidents which are later paralleled. Sometimes events are foreshadowed, such as the fight between Farfrae and Henchard's men which rehearses the fight between their masters. Sometimes they provide a mystery to be solved, as in the different descriptions of Elizabeth-Jane's eyes and hair. At other times they provide a contrast which helps to flesh out attitudes and characters, or act as a stimulus to action, as in the two entertainments put on by Farfrae and Henchard: the dismissal of Farfrae from Henchard's employment springs from this event.

A list of pairings follows. See if you can add any others to it.

Two auctions for Henchard
He auctions his wife and child (Ch 1); his possessions are auctioned (Ch 31)

Two sales as a background
The sale of horses at Weydon-Prior fair is a background to Henchard auctioning his wife (Ch 1); the hiring fair at Casterbridge where men sell their services is a background to Farfrae's and Lucetta's meeting (Ch 23)

Two birds
A swallow is trapped in a tent as Henchard auctions his wife and daughter (Ch 1); a caged goldfinch is Henchard's present to Elizabeth-Jane on her wedding day (Ch 45)

Two lots of five guineas
This is the sum paid by Newson for Susan and Elizabeth-Jane (Ch 1); it is also the sum given to Susan by Henchard on her return (Ch 10)

Two meetings at the Ring
Henchard meets Susan at the Ring (Ch 11); Henchard meets Lucetta there (Ch 35)

Two marriages for Farfrae
Farfrae marries Lucetta (Ch 29); and marries Elizabeth-Jane (Ch 44)

Two marriages for Henchard
He marries Susan twice: the second time in Ch 13

Two mayors
Henchard becomes mayor in Ch 5; Farfrae in Ch 34

Two Elizabeth-Janes
Henchard's (Ch 1); Newson's (Ch 19)

Two processions
The skimmington ride (Ch 37); the royal visit (Ch 37)

Two badly sealed letters
Susan's discloses Elizabeth-Jane's true father (Ch 19); Lucetta's discloses her relationship with Henchard (Ch 35)

Two seedsman's shops
Offered by the council but withdrawn (Ch 34); offered by the council and accepted (Ch 42)

Two fights
Between Farfrae and Henchard's employees (Ch 27); between Henchard and Farfrae (Ch 36)

Two singing sessions
Farfrae at the Three Mariners (Ch 8); Henchard at the Three Mariners (Ch 33)

Two hirings, two firings
Henchard hires Farfrae as manager (Ch 9) and Jopp as manager (Ch 26); Henchard fires Farfrae (Ch 16) and Jopp (Ch 26)

Two entertainments
Farfrae's and Henchard's (Ch 16)

Two bridges
A weather-stained brick bridge is frequented by those of 'lowest character'; a stone bridge is frequented by 'bankrupts and hypochondriacs' (Ch 32)

Two Walks
Chalk Walk is where Henchard offered Farfrae the position as his manager (Ch 9); West Walk is where Farfrae held his entertainment (Ch 16)

Two November marriages
Susan and Henchard remarry (Ch 13); Elizabeth-Jane and Farfrae marry (Ch 44)

Two Septembers
Henchard holds centre sway at the auction of his wife (Ch 1); Henchard presides as mayor at a dinner (Ch 5)

Two sets of eyes
Elizabeth-Jane has 'black eyes' (Ch 1), and 'aerial-grey' eyes (Ch 10)

Two visitors to Jersey
Henchard and Jopp

Two visits to the Fair
Henchard auctions Susan and Elizabeth-Jane at the Fair (Ch 1); Susan and Elizabeth-Jane visit the Fair when they return in search of Henchard (Ch 3)

Two visitors to Casterbridge on their way to Bristol
Farfrae (Ch 6); and Lucetta (Ch 18)

Henchard's corn
Saved by Farfrae (Ch 7); misrepresented by his employee (Ch 31)

The town band celebrates
The mayor's civic dinner (Ch 4); Lucetta and Farfrae's marriage (Ch 29)